DETERMINATION
ការតស៊ូ

A Cambodian Family's Journey

By Makna Men
and
Michael J. Vieira, Ph.D.

THE Ⓥ GROUP
Swansea, Massachusetts

Special thanks to Bill Bosi for helping with the final edits.

Text and titles set in Times New Roman.

Cover Design by Jill Carrico.

A publication of The V Group, 4 Lewin Lane, Swansea, MA 02777.

Manufactured in the United States of America.

First Edition.

ISBN: 978-1-329-66442-5

This book is dedicated to

My mother, Tha Chhun

My wife, Samoutta

My four children, Makthra, Marina, Kanika and Nicsaii

My brothers Marin, Marith, Ka, and Ra.

They have made me a stronger person

And for that I thank them.

From this point forward,

may your life be filled with happiness.

Introduction

Inside the secure, concrete, public B.M.C. Durfee High School building in Fall River, Massachusetts, this book first took shape. It was the Nineties. A lifetime away from the Seventies.

Makna Men had survived the Vietnam War and escaped from his native Cambodia. He and his family lived in fairly poor conditions even long before they walked through the killing fields and lived in refugee camps, ending up in New England.

In a way, I also survived the Vietnam War. Even though my draft lottery number was 14, my blood pressure and family history helped me escape a probable military assignment in Southeast Asia.

To be honest, I didn't feel guilty at the time. The Vietnam War was a bad thing.

As the son of a World War II veteran who, truth be told, arrived in Japan after the war was over, I did have a sense of duty and service to my country. But not to the insanity that was Vietnam.

Hell no, I wasn't going to go. Dad wasn't happy, but I agreed that I would join the draftees and the protesters, the pot smokers and the drunks who surrounded and boarded the bus that left from the Post Office in Fall River to go for my draft physical in a brick building in Boston straight out of Alice's Restaurant.

My good friend, Chuck, the conscientious objector, and I took our seats on the smoke-filled school bus with our Grateful Dead-like new pals. After a day in Boston where, as Arlo said, I was poked and prodded, injected and inspected, I was told my blood pressure was too high.

They reviewed my medical history and after learning that my grandfathers died of sudden heart attacks, the good doctors spared me a trip to Vietnam and restored peace to our home. As time went on, the whole experience did leave me with some guilt that I was able to stay in a good place, go to college and move on with life.

Makna wasn't so lucky. He was not only living in a very bad place, but he had no choice but to try to survive and to escape. He did, and I'm glad. If not, there would be no story to follow these words.

Years later, as we worked together at B.M.C. Durfee High School of Fall River and later down the street at Bristol Community College, his story and the dream of a book would come up. Sometimes we'd work on it and sometimes we'd just talk about it.

But the story and the need to tell it remained strong. For both of us, I think, it was important to put his lifelong journey into words as a way to share it with future generations. It is our hope that maybe somebody will learn from it and become more aware of the victims that war creates and the lives it destroys.

TO BE HONEST, Makna put a face on the war I thought I'd escaped. Although I had friends and family who went to Vietnam and returned changed, addicted, maimed or in a black body bag, Makna was my ghost of the past, present and future.

He reminded me of the thousands of Cambodians and other Southeast Asians who, without really being part of the political struggle, had to deal with the consequences. And, as a colleague, he taught me about his culture, his food and his faith.

In the Eighties, Makna's family often joined mine in our backyard and occasionally on a Cape Cod adventure. My family joined his for graduation parties. There were good times.

More recently, there was also unbearable pain. As this book was being readied to go to print, his son Makthra died in a tragic car accident. Ironically, I was with Makthra on the morning of his death.

Our last words were mine. He had to get his act together, I told him, and to get to work on what was due for the class I was teaching for Wentworth Institute of Technology. As my student, Makthra was often late with his work – if it came at all.

His job required long hours and he was a hard-working kid. I know that Makna had even more discussions with him that focused on his school/work conflicts. I also know that Makthra knew that Makna loved him completely and that my words were rooted in concern and caring.

Still, it would be nice to have parted on a better note. I always call my students my "kids" and they're not supposed to die.

But life isn't always nice. Sometimes it's painful and terrible. It can be unfair and cruel. To be honest, I don't know how Makna and Samoutta cope with losing a son. I don't know how I would.

The love of family, friendships and wonderful memories must be the instruments that provide comfort. Love finds a way, I guess. A cliché, maybe, but I have to believe it's true.

Then again, as Makna tells the story of his going without food, sleeping on bare floors, living in the jungle, or pulling painful leeches from his body and following unknown trails into unknown lands, I stop and just marvel at the determination that he and his family had.

His strength and that of his brothers, supported by an amazingly strong mother, is a remarkable story. Unfortunately, it's not that unique. There were many Maknas. Some live alongside us now, and others are buried in Cambodian mud.

This story is shared to honor the memory of them all.

NOW, ALMOST 30 years later, we felt a need to include some brief historical and geographic notes in Makna's story. Most come from Wikipedia or other basic sources and are intended to provide some context.

There are also some photos that give a glimpse into the Men family. They help put a face on the struggle.

For many readers, this story is ancient history – for many others, it will be a painful reminder. For everybody, I hope it provides encouragement and a lesson in life. My father used to say, "From the time you're born, 'til you're riding a hearse, things are never so bad that they couldn't get worse."

I've thought about that saying many times when I was not happy with the situation that I was in, and it made me appreciate what I had and how little many others had by comparison. Reading Makna's story should provide a similar lesson.

For most of us, just thinking about surviving the infamous "killing fields" is nearly impossible to imagine. But they were real and they provide a real lesson today when immigrants are often demonized and some people just want to make more and more money on the backs of the poor.

Life isn't fair. The story of the Men family proves that. But the United States can and should be a refuge where immigrants can work hard, raise families, and become successful. Sometimes, as generations pass, these lessons are forgotten.

Makthra and I talked about the possibility of his writing an Epilogue for this book. A reflection on the lessons of a father and the dreams of a son. Sadly, that didn't happen, but his brief life touched many people and drives home the lesson: You never know when your last day of life will be.

Savor the life you have and share the gifts you've received. That's really the moral of Makna's story. So, read this and remember that there are many survivors out there – some never went to war, some did and never came back, and some, like Makna have lived to tell a story of determination, love and strength. It's a story that needs to be shared.

Michael J. Vieira, Ph.D.

Preface

There were no birthday cakes or parties. No celebrations of our births. In fact, I don't even know when I was born.

In Cambodia, unlike in the West, birthdays are not a big event. I think I was born in 1964, and I suppose that the birth certificates that were kept at the city hall would document that – if they survived the war.

But there was another reason why many of us do not know our real birthdates. When we were in the refugee camp in Thailand, the message passed from refugee to another refugee.

"Lower your age so you can go to school," they said.

For this reason, many people made the birthdays reflect the age required so their children can go to school once they get here. My family was no exception.

It actually was not really a lie because many parents and children did not know their real birthdays. So, it was easy for parents to make up a date.

When they arrived in the USA, many parents, including my mother, honestly thought that I was born in a different year than she gave to me when we were in the refugee camp. Even if they knew the year, they were not sure of the exact day and month.

At the time, getting into school was so important, they didn't realize what difference it would make later. Today, there are Khmer and other refugees who lowered their ages as much as 10 years. Now, many of them realize that they will have to continue to work well past their retirement ages because of what took place in the refugee camps.

In my case, the only thing that my mother could go by was when she got married. I was born in 1964, one year after my parents married in 1963. My mother said it was 1964, but honestly, it was not important to remember our birthdays because they were not celebrated. With so much unforeseen turmoil in life, it was even less important for those of us in Cambodia to keep those dates in mind.

Even today, it is not important to me at all. It is just another day.

What I do remember is how much my mother loved us. Now that I'm a parent, I realize that, as parents, you love your children unconditionally. Parents will do anything to protect their children and surround their children with love.

In my case, my mother's love toward all of her children was unconditional. She made sure that we lived through the turmoil and suffering in Cambodia. Her thoughts and ability to foresee the future were remarkable. She kept all of her children alive through many hardships. This was more important than anything else.

When I was a young boy, I recall that my life was filled with happiness. I spent the day playing with other children, and, as children should be, free of worries. I remembered speaking both Chinese and Khmer. While we played, my mother was home, but my father was working at the cement factory.

My parents: Men Pon and Tha Chhun

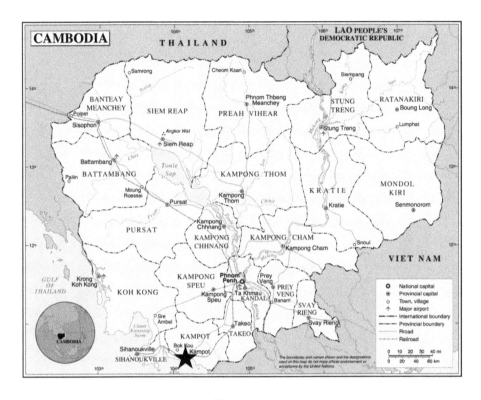

Kampot

Located in southern Cambodia not far from the Gulf of Thailand, Kampot, also known as Krong Kampot, is the capital of the Kampot Province. It is known for its black pepper, fish sauce and "the king of fruits," durian, which has been called both pleasant and sweet – and overpowering and disgusting.

1

My name is Makna Men. I do not remember very much as a child growing up in Kampot, except for a few moments.

I was born in the Province of Kampot, which is located in southern Cambodia near the Gulf of Thailand. The village has eighty Kilometers of coastal strip along the Gulf of Thailand.

Because we grew up near the coast, I spent a great deal of time along the shore, fishing and catching shrimp with handmade devices. I can still see myself standing in waist-deep, clear blue water and seeing shrimp swimming by. With the device I made, I would hook them.

As a child, I was excited that I actually caught something using what I made. I took my catch home and my mother cooked them for me. I recall that the freshly caught wild shrimp was delicious. Whenever I had spare time and was not doing chores, I was there along the ocean shores, catching shrimp and fish. Maybe that explains why I love fishing today.

Although it's been many years, I sometime find myself reflecting on my childhood, and those times running around with other children in the village. Like most kids, we played hide and seek, but we also played other Khmer traditional games.

One of the traditional games we played was called *leak kanseng* or "Hide the Scarf." The game is played by a group of children sitting in a circle in a way that is similar to the American game, "Duck, Duck, Goose."

Someone holding a "kanseng" or scarf walks around the circle while singing a song:

> *Leak Kanseng!*
> *Chhma khaaim keng!*
> *Oh long oh long*

Wayne Potash provided this translation:
Hide the scarf!
The cat is biting his/her heel
and drags the leg

While singing the song, the child secretly places the "kanseng" behind one of the children. If that chosen person realizes what is happening, he or she must pick up the "kanseng" and gently beat the person sitting next to him or her with it.

That person then runs around the circle until he or she comes to the opening spot. The person with the "kanseng" starts the process over again.

My parents did not have to worry much about me because I was a well-disciplined child. I recall that I never asked my parents for anything and I occupied myself with activities. My parents were not rich.

My childhood in Kampot was short. I remember that, but I cannot remember what village we lived in or even what our house looked like. I do remember that a truck came by to pick up my father to work.

I am not sure how long we stayed in the village or commune in Kampot before we moved closer to the factory. I think the reason for the move was that the factory needed to be operational at all times and workers had to move. Whatever the reason was, I enjoyed a brief moment in life as a child during that time.

MY FAMILY HAD A WONDERFUL LIFE near the factory. Everyone who lived around us was very friendly. We never had to worry about hurting each other. In fact, when we lived at the housing project, my family had the most money. I am not sure how, but everyone seemed to come by and borrow from my parents.

My parents always gave it to them. Sometimes they paid back on time and some still owe my parents to this day. It does not matter now because many of them are probably dead.

The housing project that we lived in was provided by the factory. It was very close to the factory, but far enough from the Kampot province. I am not sure of the distance, but it was close enough that I could get to the factory.

All of the houses were built in rows. There were six rows, and the backs of the houses in one row were close to the backs of the houses in other rows. This meant the front yards faced the other houses from another row. In each row, there were nine units. One family lived in each unit.

The house was simple. The floors throughout the houses were smooth, level cement. The framework of the house was built of wood. The roofs were covered with corrugated sheets. Each unit contained a kitchen and sleeping quarters. On our bamboo beds, we had mattresses to sleep on. There were mosquito nets over each bed. It was a nice and comfortable house.

The bathroom was separate from the living quarters. We had to share the bathroom with three other families. We also had to share the common dirt playground strip in front of each house.

All of the workers who lived in this housing project worked in shifts. There were three shifts and everyone took turns working so the factory never closed. Despite the conditions and hard work, the people that lived there built a community. Everyone knew each other and helped each other.

There was never a dull moment. There was always something going on in the project. My mother did not work. She stayed home, cleaned the house, did the cooking and took care of my brothers and me.

I remember that sometimes my father went to work at night and sometimes he went to work in the daytime. Although my father did many jobs from the time he began working in 1963, by the time he received his official identification card on April 3, 1972, his job was to sample the water.

I am not sure why he needed to sample the water. And even though I spent some precious times with him in the factory and witnessed first-hand what he did, I never understood his job, but I appreciated his hard work to support all of us.

Many times in my childhood, I would sneak out of the house to see him at night. I enjoyed doing it. My mother did not know because she was sleeping. I tiptoed to the door and got out. I never closed it behind me, because I did not want to wake my mother up. In the middle of the night, I ran by myself to the factory. It did not take very long.

When I got to the patrol gate, the guard escorted me to see my father. After several times of doing this, my father asked the guards to bring me home as soon as they saw me, but when I got home, I did not go into the house. I went around the housing project to see people playing games and dancing.

I treasure those moments in my memories.

The most common game that people played there was *bool*, which is similar to bocce. Even in the middle of the night, I still could find people playing it in front of my house. They ran electrical wires from the house to the playground and connected a light bulb to a pole to shine on the playing area.

Sometimes, I went to see people do the *Rom Vong*, a Cambodian traditional dance. Other times, I just sat in front of the house waiting for my father to come home. When he arrived, he usually brought me dessert. Most of the time that meant sweet cakes. If he did not bring a treat, he usually went into the chicken coop behind the house to catch a hen to cook in the middle of the night.

At this time of night, the women did not do the cooking – the men did the cooking instead. It was fun for me to see all of these activities and I enjoyed the times with my father. The men usually cooked the chicken in my kitchen and made chicken rice soup. I think that was all my father and his friends knew how to make.

It was a wonderful time, but in this nice, peaceful place, peace did not last!

2

It was probably sometime around 1970 when life changed for all of us at the cement factory. I started to see the first of many battles between Lon Nol's soldiers and the Communist Khmer Rouge troops. On the Khmer Rouge side, I think they had the Viet Cong (Vietnamese Communists) helping them, because many of the soldiers were Vietnamese. Although Lon Nol was the Prime Minister of Cambodia from 1970 to 1975, the Khmer Rouge Rebels won many battles. Lon Nol's soldiers usually had to re-group, and then try to recapture what had been lost.

My family got caught in the middle of several battles, and I saw many battles first hand inside the cement factory. There were a lot of casualties on both sides. Bombs and bullets did not discriminate between civilians and soldiers.

In addition to the fighting between the Khmer Rouge and Lon Nol troops, we had to face another problem: robbery by the Vietnamese. They took our money, gold, clothes, sewing machines, and whatever else they could get their hands on. I remember my mother crying and hearing her beg them not to hurt us.

They were like bandits who came through town and stole everything in sight. I did not understand why everyone was trying to hurt us.

I remembered asking my mother why the Khmer Rouge kept on trying to capture the factory, but my mother did not know the answer either. The only thing this factory produced was cement. It did not look important.

Could it be that the Khmer Rouge was trying to cripple the economy in this province? There was no one there who really knew the Khmer Rouge's intentions.

From 1970 on, the fighting started to get worse all around the factory. Each family in the housing project dug trenches to hide in, and my family was no different. My family dug our trench in an area away from our house. The reason that my father dug it there and not near the house was because there was no space closer.

The trench was dug in an open space in a grassy area. After he completed digging, he built a hut on top of it. The trench was dug in an "L" shape. Above it, he placed logs. On top of the logs, he placed palm leaves and then dirt. I helped my father dig the trench even though I was probably only about six years old. But I was the oldest son.

By 1970, I had two little brothers: Marin and Marith. They were five and two years old, I think.

My father told us that he dug this hideout in an "L" shape so everyone could move to the other half if someone fired guns into it or tossed a grenade at us from the entrance. This could save our lives.

For my brothers and me, the hut and trench became our playhouse. We danced and sang with our friends and played hide and seek there. Although it was fun for us, our parents encouraged us to play there just in case fighting began. This way all of us could easily hide in the trench and be safe. The children's safety came first in our parents' eyes.

Whenever fighting broke out around the factory, my family ran into our trench to hide. The whole housing project became very quiet. The only noises that could be heard outside were the wind, the explosion of bombs that dropped, and the guns firing. The battle usually lasted for a few hours. When it stopped, we came out and went back to our houses.

But the quiet didn't last for long.

THERE WERE MANY TIMES IN 1970 when the fighting intensified. When that happened, my family was asked to leave the housing project and to go to live inside the factory.

Once inside the factory, all of the men had to take up arms not only to defend the factory but also to protect their family members. I remember that my father had a gun. It was an old gun. I now think it was a carbine.

I held onto it. The rifle was longer than me.

My father carried that weapon with him to patrol around the factory with some other men. The fighting was always between Lon Nol's soldiers and the Khmer Rouge. For about two years, there was no major fighting around the factory, but all workers were asked to hold on to their guns in case of an attack by the Khmer Rouge.

Probably in 1972, the Khmer Rouge launched a major attack on the factory. The fighting must have lasted at least fifteen hours. It was the most frightening experience I ever encountered as a child. The battle was so close to us and the worst part of the experience was that my father was not there. He was working in another building.

It never seemed to end.

I heard loud sounds so close and people were screaming from bullet wounds. I could not stop but wonder if the screams for help were coming from my father?

I cried.

We stayed in one location because it was the most protected area. The battle continued into the night and I remember that it was in the middle of the night when my mother woke all of us up. It was so dark because the electricity was out. Quietly, my mother whispered into our ears to get our shoes, but we did not have the chance to do even that.

I do not think my mother had slept at all that night. She stayed awake the whole time to monitor the situation outside. As soon as she thought that it was getting worse and we were not safe, she moved all of us out. In those tense moments, I followed my mother's directions.

For a change, I did not give her any attitude. I listened to her and assisted her in any possible way to help her get us out of the situation we were in. We left the room and went down the hall to go down through a manhole which led to a dark, open space under the building. We hid down there with a few other families.

When the fighting stopped, we came out and went outside. The sun was so bright.

IN THE DAYLIGHT, I saw that a lot of buildings had been destroyed. Suddenly, the Khmer Rouge came to get us and took us to another building in the factory. I met my father there, but the Khmer Rouge had tied him up.

Each family was allowed to sit next to their loved ones. They kept every man tied up for many hours in this building, and none of us were given any food or water.

All of the men had their legs tied together. They were also tied at their elbows, and their arms were pulled toward their backs. They were treated like animals.

To this day, I still have the image of my father tied up sitting with all of us waiting for his fate. It was so painful to watch, but it has become even more painful to remember after many years passed. It is part of the scar that war left on me and my family – but especially for my mother.

The soldiers stood around just watching us, and celebrating their victory. They opened up Coca-Cola bottles and they drank in front of us. They would not share it with any of us. They treated us like we were combat enemies.

We were not.

My father and other people around us were civilian workers, who were working in the cement factory to support their families. They were not soldiers

Even though each man in the factory was given a gun to protect himself, none of them were trained to fight. They were not in military uniforms. Each of these men including my father, had their families around them.

It was clear that we were not the enemy.

My brothers were thirsty, and my mother was begging the soldiers for water, but they ignored her. We were there for many hours, just sitting hunched together in a room.

They did not say much to any of us, but they treated every one of us like we were criminals. Many hours passed by, and all of us just sat there and sweated. No one knew what they planned to do with us.

AS I LOOKED AROUND THROUGH THE WINDOWS, I saw many buildings around me had been destroyed. The walls were down and the ceilings had fallen. Blocks of cement were scattered and glass was shattered everywhere.

Gun shots could still be heard in and outside the factory. Through the windows, I saw a few people shooting at each other.

Many hours went by and the fighting seemed to be a little bit quieter. I was hoping that when the fighting was over, the Khmer Rouge would untie my father. In that quiet, hope-filled moment, the soldiers disappeared from the building. I was wondering what had happened.

My family wanted to leave, but we were afraid. We hesitated at first because no one knew what to do. After a while, my mother untied my father. One by one, people from the other families also did the same. The workers slowly stood up. But then, there was big bang.

As we were getting up to leave, something exploded on top of the building. We were being shot at from the nearby mountain top. Everyone scrambled to hide, like mice in a maze, but there was no place to go.

We were trapped in a room.

With no place to go, we just sprawled out on the floor. Each family laid flat on the cement floor when the blasts hit. Between the explosions, people ran out of the room into other rooms to hide. Every family tried to find a safe place and ran for cover. My family was no exception.

We did not know which group was firing at us, but whatever group it was, we knew we were the target. The intention was to kill.

Whoever they were, they put a red flag on top of the building as a signal to command their battery to aim toward the building. I saw three shells from the battery hit the building. It penetrated the roof a little, and it sent down dust and cement on top of our heads.

My family ran for cover.

WE WEREN'T ALONE. There were people running in all directions.

Even though we found a place to hide, no one knew if it was safe. All of us were scared stiff.

When we were in the room, my father began moving the furniture. He was a brave man, who struggled to protect his family. Unlike the rest of us, he did not hide. *Lok Pha*, translated as Dad, pushed chairs and tables to block the door to stop the debris from getting into the room.

Just as we were settled in, the room opposite us was directly hit. The wind and the debris splashed into our room and into the hallway. When the next airplane came by, it hit our room. We were scattered all over the room, hiding in every corner.

As for me, I put my head into a drawer and cried. When I looked up, there was a big hole in the ceiling.

I could barely see my parents and my brothers in the room. There was a lot of dust and everywhere was chaos. To be honest, I thought I had lost my parents and my brothers. Thank Lord Buddha, they were all right.

Many people cried, including me, because we were scared. I did not know how we survived that blast, but we did. The steel construction of the building was hanging from the roof. The furniture that my father had put up against the door was blown away. The families in the room in front of us did not make it.

Maybe it was not our time.

The cement factory in Kampot.

3

When the fighting was over, there was only a small group of people who came out of their rooms into the hallway. About thirty people died.

We were lucky.

The only person in my family who was hurt was my brother Marin. He had a cut on his face from the bomb fragments. Today, almost forty years later, the scar is still visible on his face.

As we were coming out of our hiding place, other families also came out. At that moment, as people rushed out of hiding, the crowd pushed me away from my parents. I tried so hard to get back to them, but people kept on pushing me further away. I heard my parents' voices but I could not get to them.

I was so scared. I did not know what to do. I cried. I kept on calling for my parents and my parents kept on yelling for me. I think I was eight years old.

At that moment, another air raid struck the same building. This one, however, did not hit us directly. It hit the same building, but not right on top of us.

Everyone laid down except me. I was standing. My parents and I were about twenty feet away from each other. My father came quickly and grabbed me.

We left that building and headed out of the factory. As we walked out, we saw many buildings had been destroyed and we saw many bodies buried in the rubble. This fighting was the biggest battle since the factory had come to existence that I could recall.

Later, I learned that the bombs that dropped on us were from Lon Nol's soldiers. Their intention was to kill the Khmer Rouge soldiers, but there were no soldiers inside the building. The only people who were trapped in the building were civilians, and we became the target.

All the Khmer Rouge soldiers and the Viet Cong had left the premises. Maybe the soldiers had no way of knowing who was inside the building. Whatever the intention was, many families lost their love ones.

We walked through the factory in our bare feet. We tried to navigate through the broken glass, bomb fragments, cement blocks that once were part of the building, and the dead and injured bodies. Finally, we managed to get out. It took us a couple of days to realize the pain our feet were in from the glass and metal shreds we stepped on during our exit.

Once out of the factory, we started our journey through rice paddies and began heading back to Kampot province. There were many times that we were not sure if we would ever make it back to the city.

On our way to the main road, we encountered three patrol groups. In each patrol group, there were three or four soldiers. They were Lon Nol soldiers who were waiting outside the factory. We were stopped and questioned, but I did not know what they were questioning us about. I do not know what my father said to them, but we safely passed them.

We walked through many rice fields and farms to get to the main road that lead us to Kampot. When we reached the main road, we saw a man in a three-wheeled motorcycle. My father convinced him to drive us the rest of way to Kampot.

ONCE WE ARRIVED AT THE CITY, we had to find a place to stay. My father bought a house. The house was not big, but it was good enough for the family. The roof and the walls of this house were covered with palm leaves.

Our family was able to spend a lot of time together for a few months before the factory reopened. It was during this time that my father taught me some French.

When the factory opened, my father went back to work, but we did not move into the factory with him. He and the other people who went back to work in the factory were trucked in. The trucks were similar to those that the army used to carry soldiers to the battle field.

While my father was at work, the government ordered my mother and other women to make sharp bamboo traps for the army. I remember seeing my mother carving sharp points on bamboo sticks for Lon Nol's

24

government. Every day a government worker came by each house to collect them.

One day in late 1973 or early 1974, it was my father's turn to go to work, but he was sick and he asked someone else to take his place. That night a vigorous battle took place at the factory between Lon Nol's army and the Khmer Rouge.

Many people died and many trucks came back to the city with bodies. Most of the people who died were factory workers. Those who survived were stuck inside the factory.

Thank Lord Buddha, my father was not there to see it or to experience it. I think the fighting continued for many more days, and I still remembered seeing the smoke and hearing the sound of explosions.

At about the same time, the fighting intensified around Kampot as well. My father decided to send all of us back to Phnom Penh, the capital city of Cambodia, but we ended up in Prey Veng Province, which was the birth place of my father and mother.

From 1970 to 1975, which really was all of my childhood life, I was always on the move in an attempt to escape the gun fights and close encounters in the battlefields. I never stayed in one place long enough to get a good education and to make friends.

My teenager years were stolen from me. Unlike my children and most of my friends, I never knew what it meant to be a teenager. From the time I can remember, I had to become a grown up.

There was nothing else to do in order to survive. That is what war does. It strips down your childhood and changes your life in the blink of an eye.

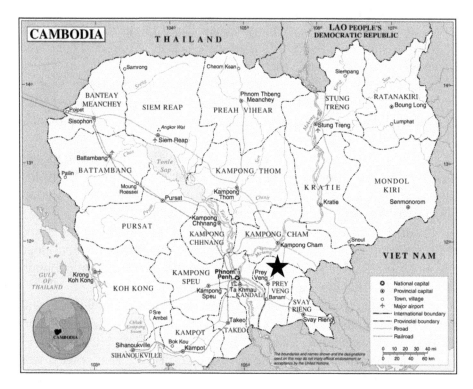

Prey Veng

Prey Veng means "long forest" in Khmer, but by 1975 when the Khmer Rouge took power, what once was a splendid wooded region was deforested and used for agricultural. Despite its richness, the province experienced its first famine from 1975-1977 and became the site of mass graves for thousands of people who were killed by the Khmer Rouge.

4

When we arrived at Prey Veng, the situation there seemed to be normal at first. At least, there was no fighting. I believe we lived at my father sister's home because I remember spending a great deal of time with my first cousins, Kea and Sok. While we were moving around, we also spent some time at my grandmother's home.

Both houses were not big, but at least it was home.

Like most of the houses, the home I remember most was built about eight feet above the ground, because this area always flooded. The frame of the house was made of wood. The roof and the walls were made of palm leaves. The floor was made of boards, but the ground under the house was dirt.

During the day, if people took a bath inside their houses, the water seeped through the floors and sprinkled to the ground below. That was actually a good thing. It helped to wet the dirt so that it would not be too dusty. All of the people who lived in that area were not wealthy, but they were happy, and that was important.

I enjoyed going to the rice field with my grandmother and my mother very much. Sometimes my uncle and aunt took me around the village, which was not a big one.

In the village, all of the houses were also above ground. All of the streets were dirt roads. There were no paved roads. Most of the people who lived in this village were farmers. There were a few businessmen, but all they wanted to do was to buy rice from people there.

The people were very friendly. Everyone knew each other. We often shared meals and food with one another. When there was a problem, we helped each other out – especially during the harvesting and planting seasons.

The land that these farmers worked had been passed on from their families for many generations. My grandmother, for example, received her land from her parents and was prepared to pass it on to my parents.

Just as the land was passed from generation to generation, so were the farming techniques. They used a cow to plow the fields. Then they worked the soil with a hoe and a metal rake to clear the grass from the field. Cow manure was spread for fertilizer.

Usually the planting involved the whole family and sometimes the neighbors also helped. In order to get the land ready to plant rice, all of the people had to work very hard. One job was managing the irrigation. Sometimes they raised the land to stop the water from going to the next field. If the land was too wet, they used buckets and, at times, machinery to level the water in the field.

Planting rice involved a lot of time and skill. Once the rice was fully grown, it still needed care because crabs could destroy the rice stems if they were not watched carefully. When it was time to harvest, even more care was needed, because the birds came in flocks to eat the rice. Farmers used nets to trap the rice birds.

The rice fields were very big. Some rice fields covered a couple of acres and some families owned two to three rice fields. The rice fields were also always muddy. The only time that they dried up was during the harvesting season and immediately after.

Farmers started working on their land a couple of months after the harvest. Usually, the best time to start was after a major rainfall. First, they plowed, leveled and cleared the field of any unwanted weeds or grass. Once the rice was planted, the farmers had to bring water into the fields by irrigation.

Some crops took about three months to grow, but other crops took as long as five months before harvesting. When the rice was ready, the field turned from green to orange.

When the harvesting season started in late March or early April, the ground became dry. It was during this time that I had a lot of fun in the rice fields chasing birds and watching people harvest their rice.

There were a lot of birds looking for loose rice in the fields. Most of them were successful because the birds were very fat. We called those birds "rice birds" and we ate them. They were delicious.

After the feathers were plucked off, the rice birds were the size of a human thumb. People marinated them and deep fried them until they were crispy. You could eat them whole – and I did!

In 2012, I took my wife and my twin children to Cambodia. My youngest son, Nicsaii tried the rice birds and he loved them as much as I did when I was about his age. That was one of the memorable thing of the trip. I told him that daddy used to eat them as well when I was a young boy.

I think that harvesting was the most difficult and dangerous part of farming especially for someone like me who did not know how to do it.

The farmers used sickles to cut the rice stems. They grabbed a handful each time and cut them close to the base. As they moved through the fields, they placed the rice stems on the ground as they went. After they cut a lot of them, they came back, gathered the stems and tied them up. Once they had a lot of them tied up, they put them on the cart and oxen pulled it to the village.

After the rice was back in the village, the farmers hit the rice stems against a board to separate the rice. Then they let it dry which yielded the rice grain. Some of the farmers could afford a rice grinding machine.

In July of 2015, the oxen are still pulling carts. Nicsaii rode one during a visit to my village, Prey Sla in Prey Pnov Commune, Prey Veng Province. (Photo by Makna Men.)

5

As I was enjoying my life growing up in Prey Veng, the war was going on in Vietnam. It was probably in the late Sixties or early Seventies at that time, so the situation was not good.

I remember seeing the Vietnamese soldiers crossing the border to stay under my grandmother's house when the bombs dropped along the border. Because her house was raised up on stilts above the ground, the Vietnamese soldiers used to tie their hammocks to the poles beneath her house and sleep.

We were not afraid of the men. In fact, sometimes it was fun. Occasionally, the soldiers asked me to play games with them. They also put me on their laps and often swung me around.

At the time, this was a normal part of my childhood for me. I did not know the difference between soldiers and the other adults. There was not much of a separation between family friends and military foe. In fact, it did not matter much to me that soldiers were part of my daily life because all of my childhood in Cambodia was marked by one conflict after another. It became what we considered to be normal.

One day, above the sky in the distance, I saw an airplane dropping these things from the belly of the craft. Soon afterward, I heard an explosion, but I did not know where it came from. There was a lot of noise.

When the sounds of the explosions stopped, the soldiers untied their hammocks and they walked away.

Each day, the soldiers did the same thing. They may have gone back to Vietnam to stay with their families or they may have gone back to fight the Americans. The funny thing was that, through it all, I was not scared, maybe because I was never harmed in any way.

Day by day, the situation seemed to get worse.

The soldiers kept on coming to our province more frequently, and as a result, the bombs kept getting closer to where we lived. Many people packed their bags and left their homes.

One day, one of my relatives, named Ang, came to the province and took all of us to Phnom Penh. I remember that it was a difficult trip from Prey Veng to Phnom Penh.

We travelled during the flooding season, so there was a lot of water covering the dirt road and filling the potholes. We were riding on a motorcycle and whenever we hit a pothole, we fell off and landed in the water. That didn't stop us. We just got up again and kept on riding until we reached the capital. It was the journey of a lifetime.

Lon Nol, second from left, with U.S. Vice President Spiro Agnew during a state visit to Cambodia in 1970. Photo by Dara.

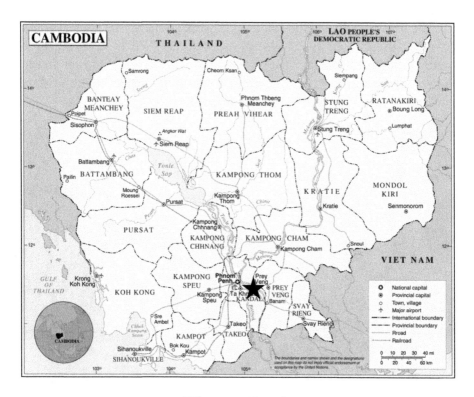

Phnom Penh

The capital and largest city in Cambodia, Phnom Penh was founded in 1434. In the 1920s, it was considered the most beautiful French-built city and was once called the "Pearl of Asia." During the Vietnam War, the city was flooded with refugees who made up most of its two to three million residents by 1975. The Khmer Rouge cut off supplies to the city for more than a year before it fell on April 17, 1975. The entire population of the city was evacuated in what has been called a "death march" and forced to do labor on rural farms. The Khmer Rouge was driven out of Phnom Penh in 1979 and in the decades after the war, returned to its prominence as not only Cambodia's wealthiest and most populated city, but also a popular tourist destination.

6

Just as we were in Prey Veng for only a couple months, we did not stay in the capital for very long either. Soon, my father wanted all of us to join him back in Kampot. So we did.

But as soon as we got to Kampot, we discovered that the situation was not safe. We went back to Phnom Penh but my father stayed behind. When we arrived back in Phnom Penh, we stayed with relatives. We had nothing left, except for some clothing. Except for a brief period in Kampot, we never even had our own home.

In Phnom Penh, we stayed with my first cousin on my mother's side. She had just won the lottery and had bought a house at Phar Dam Kor with two floors. Despite the two floors, I remember where we stayed was congested.

Their house was not luxurious, but at least it was their own home. The house was constructed almost entirely of wood. On the second floor, there were even hardwood floors. The roof of the house was covered with corrugated iron roofing.

The house was located in a very busy section of the city and the streets were narrow. The house did not have any yard to play in because there were so many houses built next to each other. There was not much else to do there except eat and sleep because my father was still working at Kampot.

Although we couldn't play outside, we were not bored. My cousin bought a television from their winnings for the second floor. I liked it a lot, and every night I watched Cambodian movies. I do not recall how big the television was, but I know that I enjoyed it a great deal. It was my pastime.

My family stayed on the first floor. The first floor was not as nice as the second floor, but it was still better than all the other houses that we lived in. We had one big bed that all of us shared. The floor was cement, and in the middle of the floor, the owner had dug a ditch as a hiding place just in case there was an attack by the Khmer Rouge.

Every day we ate near the ditch just in case something might happen. Every day, we had to be careful. We never knew when the Khmer Rouge were going to unleash the shelling into the capital. One day in 1974, about six months after we had moved in, my mother was about to go to the market, but she hesitated. I do not know why. It was as if she felt that something bad was going to happen.

We were upstairs watching television, but she wanted us downstairs. She called all of us to come down to the kitchen on the first floor to eat, and so we did. Little did we know that this was the last meal that we would eat in the house.

What happened next was chaos.

7

Just as we were sitting down to eat, we heard a loud noise over the roof. It vibrated as if something was about to drop on top of our head.

A few seconds later, we heard a big explosion. We realized that it was not the wind that made the roof move.

During most of my childhood, I was living with war, but my parents moved a lot to try to provide a normal life. That's why we moved back and forth between Kampot and Prey Veng, and why my experiences with the soldiers were very different.

When I lived in my village in Prey Veng province, I played with the Vietnamese soldiers because they tied hammocks under the house and were friendly to us. But when the bomb dropped closer to the village, my cousin brought us to Phnom Penh, the capital city.

All of my childhood life, I experienced war, turmoil and constant relocation. It seemed like I had so much practice hiding from bombs and bullets, but what I was about to experience was something new. At about 10 years old, I learned what war was really like.

My mother told all of us to get into the ditch. We jumped in.

A few minutes later, there was another noise and it was followed by another explosion. Just when we thought it was over, another one came, and it landed about three houses away from us.

After those first explosions, there were two more explosions, and people started to scream for help. I could hear people moaning from pain, people losing their limbs, losing their loved ones, and just sheer fright. A lot of people cried.

My cousin's husband was confused. He dragged his motorcycle from the house and walked out. Some of the people who lived next door to us screamed at us to get out of the house.

But while some yelled, "Fire. Run!" Others told us to stay put. It was confusing. We didn't know what to do or where to go, so we just stayed together.

Soon we discovered that there was indeed a fire. Not only was it burning out of control, but the wind was also blowing in our direction. There was an inferno – and it was only a few houses away from us.

My mother told us to stay in the ditch. She ran outside to see for herself what was happening. The first thing she saw was fire. She ran back in and took all of us out of the ditch. My cousin's husband also came back into the house, and he did not take anything with him. It seemed as if he had lost his mind. He looked so sad. He was probably thinking that he dedicated all of his winnings to this house and now it was going to burn to the ground.

At first we all, including my mother, were confused. People ran in all directions. There were hundreds of people scrambling to get out of their homes and trying to leave the area. People were pushing each other in the narrow pathways to the main road.

My family was no exception. I saw a lot of people crying. Maybe they had lost their loved ones. As we pushed our way through the sea of sadness, I saw corpses and wounded people everywhere.

The explosion happened during the day and people were in their houses and in the street. The fire was now burning fiercely. The wind seemed to pick up from nowhere. The big explosion that we heard came from a gasoline station. That helped to explain why the fire was burning so rapidly.

My mother told all of us to hold on to each other's hands tightly. She held on to Ka's hand. He was the youngest and she wanted to be sure that he was close to her. As the oldest, I was the last one in line.

As we ran out, many other people pushed their way out as well. There were mobs of people in one small path. We were all so close to the fire. The wounded were left behind and burned in the fiery rubble. No one stopped to help anyone else. People shoved anybody in their way and just tried to force their way out of the war zone. We knew that only those who could fight their way out would survive.

People pushed my brothers and me against the barbed wire fence, but my mother kept on pulling us out. Yes, we were bleeding and yes we were scared, but we survived the inferno.

When my family got out to the main road, I looked back and I saw many buildings destroyed. People were hurt everywhere. The shelling also struck the market place where my mother was supposed to go. If she had gone to the market, who knows what would have happened to her, my brothers and me? It was so sad to see so many people moaning for help.

One of my uncles, who was in the Military Police, came to see what happened. He knew that we lived there, but he did not know if we had survived. When we emerged from the smoke and fire, he waited for us on the main road.

He took us to live with another relative in Tek La Ork, which was another area in the capital city of Phnom Penh. The fire continued to burn for the next few days.

MY MOTHER COULD NOT SLEEP for many days. She was so worried and concerned about the future of her family. Despite the worries, she was a strong woman. She kept all of her children alive and she did not panic.

Nak Ma Dai or mom knew exactly what she had to do. She was always prepared for any emergency. Even though we were in the capital city, she had prepared a small sack of clothing and her other important belongings. If there was an actual emergency, she knew exactly what to grab.

After this ordeal, my mother decided to send a letter to my father who still lived and worked in Kampot. She wanted him to come to Phnom Penh and to leave the job at the factory.

A few days later, my father came. For the next two to three days, my parents talked to each other about what to do next. I knew that my parents had little money left.

All of our belongings were gone. We had only a few changes of clothes. We did not have a home. And now, my father did not have a job.

My father decided to stay in Phnom Penh. With the little money that our family had, he bought an old taxi and started a taxi business, but this taxi broke down almost every day. Making a living out of this wreck of a vehicle was impossible because my father was losing money all the time.

It was then that my parents decided to move to Battambang province.

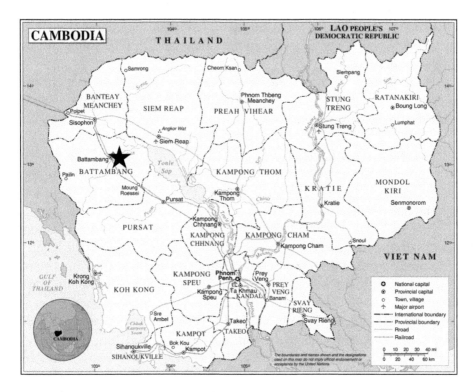

Battambang

Located in the Northwest, Battambang was founded in the 11th century by the Khmer Empire. Situated by the Sangkae River, the major commercial hub and provincial capital of what had been the Siamese province of Inner Cambodia, is known for being the leading rice-producing province in the country.

8

When we arrived at Battambang in 1974, my family had nothing left. But we still had each other and, fortunately, our relatives.

Because my immediate family did not have any money left, we ended up staying at my mother's brother's house. He was a school teacher. He had a nice wooden home at the beginning of the street.

The house had two floors, and on the first floor his wife sold everyday items like sugar, garlic, rice, and other staples. They set these items on a table underneath the house, and hung other goods from rafters of the second floor above. It was an open space and, as people went by, they would stop to buy the ingredients they needed to cook.

There were no specialty items or anything. It was just a place to get basic items that they could grab and go. There were no meats sold, but rice was available there.

Since it was not a big business, the makeshift shop was not busy at all, but my uncle's wife needed something to do to supplement her husband;s salary as a school teacher. It was also very close to a dirt road, so it was always dusty. There was a small pond in front of the house. People often discarded items in the pond, so there was always a faint smell from the heating sun.

Once in a while, people stopped by to buy stuff and they ended up talking. In the Cambodian culture, children were not allow to participate or even to hear the conversations. But it was apparent that people who lived inside the city, lived in fear – and my family was no exception.

At night, I could hear the faint noise of shelling in the distance. Battles were being fought in the countryside, but inside the city, people tried to live a normal life. But I remember my parents saying that it is only a matter of time before the Khmer Rouge take over the city.

We all stayed on the second floor with my uncle's family. There were no rooms in this house. It was just one big open space with hardwood floors. We hung cloth to make it a more private place. My family hung cloth to make a room for us, and although it was a tiny makeshift room, at least we had a roof over our head. I could not recall if we slept on the floor or on the mat, but we certainly had no mattresses. We shared the space, but not the food.

My mother had eight other siblings, and of them all, my family was the poorest. Mom was the youngest and the least educated person in her family. Even so, she did not want to place any more burdens on her brother than she had to. She was, after all, married with her own family.

Because we were poor, our meals were not like my uncle's family, so we each did our cooking and we ate separately from each other, even though each family used the same kitchen. My parents simply could not afford chicken, pork and beef. These items were just too expensive. Our meals were simple. Usually, they consisted of vegetables, but sometimes we had to eat rice porridge instead of solid rice. Even that was too expensive.

There were small yards on both sides and in back of the house. Behind the house, there were a few trees. I do not know what kind of trees they were, but the fruit was edible. In front of the house, across the dirt road, there was a small pond and I enjoyed fishing there. Just like when I was very young, it became a habit of mine. But it also was something to occupy my time.

While I fished or sat in the house and yard, I watched the neighborhood. Every day when people walked or rode their bicycles by, it was so dusty. Further along the street there were many other houses.

Although my uncle's house was not big, it was comfortable. We stayed with his family for a few months, because we could not afford to live anywhere else. Many times, my family did not even have any money to buy food. I knew that my parents borrowed money and rice from my uncle, but we could not pay him back. I am not even sure if he told his wife what he did, but I was very appreciative for his kindness.

MY FATHER LOOKED FOR A JOB, but there were no jobs to be found. I guess word got around to my mother's mother, who I think lived with her older daughter in Pailin, which was about 80 kilometers from Battambang province.

My grandmother came to see us. Once she saw how poor we were, my grandmother took off her gold neck chain and gave it to my family. She stayed with us for a while and that was the last time we saw her. She died in 1983 in Cambodia.

My parents used the money from selling the gold chain to buy a plot of land and built a house on it. It was not far from my uncle's house. The house was not big and it was not very nice either, but we were on our own.

Everything in this house was made from bamboo and palm leaves. There were no separate rooms in the building. It was all on one floor. Half of the house was the sleeping quarter, which was raised above the ground. The sleep area was made from bamboo because it was the cheapest material. The other half of the house had a dirt floor. The kitchen was separated from the living quarters by palm leaf walls, and the bathroom was outside

It was in this house that my mother gave birth to my youngest brother, Ra.

Despite the living conditions, my brothers and I managed to live a happy life. Once again, our time there was brief.

Even as a young boy, I knew the hardships my parents faced every day. I understood how hard they worked to support us and what they tried to do to give us a good life. I was not about to give them any more headaches.

Not only did I not ask for anything from them because I understood the living conditions, but I tried to help my parents as much as I could. I swept the floors and carried water from the pond to the house every day.

Besides all the chores that I had to do around the house, I took care of my brothers while my parents were out looking for work and when they were able to get jobs at some places to support us.

By the time that I was about ten years old, I had the responsibility of an adult.

9

One day, my father came home and he told us that he had found a job. He went to work very early in the morning and sometimes he did not come home until very late. From the beginning, I did not know what he was doing, and he would not tell me.

My mother also worked. She went to the market every day where she bought different kinds of tropical fruits at wholesale prices. She then tried to sell the items at market price. She acted as the "middle person," buying at a lower price and trying to sell at a higher price.

Sometimes she could not sell all of the items and they were delivered to our house. We never knew what would show up. Sometimes there was a huge pile of oranges or other tropical fruits in the middle of the house. The next day, she took the goods back out and tried to sell them again.

It was very difficult and sometimes she made only a little bit of money. If there was anything that didn't sell, we would eat it but that not only meant loss income, but it was also a little risky. Would we have food? Would it still be good?

To supplement our diet of mostly leftover food, my parents also had a little garden next to the house. There were all kinds of vegetables that grew there. My parents had a small garden, which I looked over. They planted eggplants, Chinese broccoli, lettuce, and other vegetables. It was not much, but it was helpful.

One day, my mother told me that my father was working at someone's farm. I am not sure what he did at the farm, but I assume it was whatever the owner wanted him to do. He probably plowed the fields and fed the animals. Sometimes he also had to transfer animals to the market. That was all the information she gave us.

My family did not have any transportation. The only thing the family owned was a bicycle that my father used for work every day.

Both of them worked very hard to support all of us. They never once complained that it was tough and I never saw them arguing with each other either. The war caused prices of food to go up and whenever my parents thought that they had enough cash to buy something, it went up. The inflation was high.

My family never seemed to catch a break. And it didn't get better.

WHEN MY MOTHER GAVE BIRTH to my youngest brother, she could not go to the market to buy and sell vegetables for many months. That caused so much hardship for my family. With only one income, it ended up being the most difficult time we had faced.

To supplement the lost income, my mother learned to make *Srar Sor*, which was rice wine. It was like *Saki*, but it was made in the house. It was illegal, but my mother had no choice but to do it. It was a matter of survival.

The rice wine was made in the kitchen. I am not sure how she made it or what the process of fermentation was, but I knew that the final product was very potent.

One day, an accident occurred in the kitchen.

My father was not at home, but my brothers and I were. As usual, I was watching them, including my youngest brother Ra, who was only three or four months old.

My mother was working in the kitchen. Occasionally, she would call me into the kitchen to help her. One day, she was using instruments, and mom explained to me that she was measuring the alcohol content of the wine. She said it was 100 percent alcohol.

Since I was the oldest son, I had more responsibility in the house, and often helped my parents with all kinds of chores. But sometimes my brother Marin would also try to help my mother as well.

On that day, his help really hurt.

Marin came to see my mother in the kitchen just as she was testing the alcohol. My brother lit a match.

He was only eight or nine years old, so he didn't know that the liquid was one hundred percent alcohol – or how dangerous that was near fire.

My mother did, and the flame scared her. She accidentally tipped the bottle toward herself, and in a flash my mother was instantly engulfed in flames.

She screamed for help and I did not know what to do. I ran outside to look for help, but I could not find anyone. It was a good thing that I could not find people to help my mother. If people knew that my family was making rice wine, who knew what would have happened to my mother and father. I was so scared. I ran back inside and tried to help her.

In an instant, my mother grabbed a rice bag and soaked it in water which was next to her. Mother put it on herself and the fire was extinguished. Her upper front body was burned badly.

My mother looked awful, and my brother and I didn't know how to help her or what to do. So we just stood there crying.

We just stood there, staring at her with half of her body burned. But we were thankful that she was alive. We thought for sure that the fire would burn the house down with our mother still inside. She laid on the dirt floor until my father came home late that evening.

When he got home, he was shocked by what had happened, but he did not say a word. He took his bicycle and went to buy medicine for my mother. I have no idea what medication he got, but it worked and her healing began.

At the same time that my mother's condition improved, Cambodia was about to get worse.

Harvesting rice in Battambang. Photo by Stefan Fussan.

Flag of Democratic Kampuchea. Source: Wikipedia.

Khmer Rouge

A corruption of the French term for "Red Khmers" (Khmers Rouges), this name was given to the Communist Party of Kampuchea in Cambodia. Led by Pol Pot and others, it was founded as an offshoot of the Vietnam People's Army of North Vietnam. From 1975 – 1979, they were the ruling party of Cambodia. During this time, millions of Cambodians died from widespread famine, lack of medicine, and executions. It is often remembered as the "Killing Fields" era.

10

It was April 17, 1975 when word came over the radio that the Khmer Rouge had taken over Cambodia. The country was now called Democratic Kampuchea, the name given by the Khmer Rouge, a guerrilla group driven by communist ideas. The group took root in Cambodia's northeastern jungles as early as the 1960s. The first order from the new government was that everyone must use the word *Mit*, which means "friend," toward one another.

We would now be "friends" by law? That confused or angered my people.

People were gathering in nearby groups discussing the implications of what the new government would do. Some wondered if we would have a better life now that the war was over. In other groups, people were quiet and were not sure what to do and what to expect from the Khmer Rouge.

There were a lot of uneasy feelings.

People were whispering and gossiping everywhere. In the meantime, the Khmer Rouge soldiers celebrated their victory on the streets. I could hear guns firing into the air. By late afternoon, however, the situation seemed to be reversed.

As quickly as it started, the Khmer Rouge celebration was over.

People broke up from the groups and headed back to their houses. There was a sense of concern among the people. Some people still talked about what was going to happen next, but they were mumbling.

In most of the households, including my own, there was a sense of distrust and uncertainty about the new government. No one seemed to know what to do. Some claimed that the new government was going to help them because they were poor, but others said that the Khmer

46

Rouge government had strict rules because they were a Communist government.

Even though there were a lot of words exchanged back and forth among the people, I am not even sure if people even knew what a Communist was – and that included my parents.

No one had ever lived with the Khmer Rouge, so our knowledge of the Khmer Rouge was based on hearsay. A majority of the people heard that most of the Khmer Rouge were young farmers who were poor.

The conversation among the adults was all speculation, but the guessing was soon replace with reality. On that same day, at about mid-morning, a Khmer Rouge soldier came to my house.

THE KHMER ROUGE SOLDIER was dressed in a uniform consisting of a black shirt and black pants. When I saw him, I knew he was a member of the Khmer Rouge because I had seen this uniform before when I was in Kampot.

To some of the people who lived around me, this stranger in black was new to them. But not to me. My family had run away from them before in many instances. Although I did not know everything about their politics and motives, I knew they were to be feared.

This particular soldier had his sleeves rolled up to his elbows and his pants rolled up to his knees. He had bullets strapped around his chest, and he held an AK-47 in his hand.

As he got closer to my house, we could tell that he was young – probably in his early twenties – but he looked mean and seemed to be an angry individual. In spite of his age, he was very scary.

The Khmer Rouge soldier ordered my family to leave the house. He fired his gun in front of the house. Even at my young age, it was clear that he was trying to show that he was in charge – and that he was not afraid to use his gun.

It worked.

People were panicking and my mother was one of them, mostly because my father was not home. She wasn't alone. We were all scared stiff. We did not know what to do.

But even though she was afraid, my mother stood her ground.

My mother told the soldier that she could not leave the house yet because her husband was not home. The soldier wanted to know where my father was, but my mother said that she did not know where he went.

She was telling the truth and I guess he believed her. The soldier went to a few other houses and then he came back to ours.

About half an hour later, my father came home and the soldier ordered us to get out again. He explained that we would be leaving the house for only a few days. The new government needed to re-organize the country and they did not want the people to stay in that place.

At that time, we thought he was telling the truth, but we found out that it was just an excuse that the Khmer Rouge used. Everyone seemed to believe what they said. Whether they did or not, I do not think people really had a choice.

My family packed our bag. In this bag, we had about three kilograms or about five pounds of rice and a few changes of clothes for everyone in the family. We made sure that we had the medicine for my mother.

My father put everything on his bicycle and we left the house. We did not have much to pack, because we did not have much of anything from the beginning. It was just another move for us, but this time, we did not know where to go.

The order from the Khmer Rouge was to leave the house and so we did. When we got to the main road, we met thousands of people just like us. Families and individuals who had been ordered by the new government to leave their homes.

Everyone followed one direction. And that was out of the city.

11

It was April – the dry season in Cambodia. It was hot and everyone was on foot.

The evacuation of the city took place in less than a 12 hour period. No one could tell if you were rich, middle class or poor. Looking back, in just a few hours, the Khmer Rouge had created a Communist state.

Everyone seemed to be the same – we were all walking and carrying just a few items with us.

I remember that people did not seem to have many of their belongings, because everyone thought that they would go back to their homes in a few days.

There were no cars on the street. The only moving things that I saw were bicycles, push carts and thousands of people walking.

Along the street, we saw Khmer Rouge soldiers standing guard, and occasionally, they pushed us to move forward. Everyone walked until sunset. We tried to stop and rest along the way, but the Khmer Rouge guards would not let us rest. They kept on pushing us.

Finally, the sun set and everyone was told by the Khmer Rouge to get off the road and to stay to the side. So we did, but none of the people who had left with us were now with us. Everyone was walking at different paces, and some of them were trailing behind us and some were ahead of us.

My father wanted to go back to Prey Veng to live with his parents and sister. I think my mother did not agree and that was the struggle my parents had. My father said that the war was over, and in a way, it was. Dad wanted to join his family in Prey Veng.

My mother finally gave in. We thought we would soon be okay, but what my father or any of us did not realize was that the nightmare was just about to begin.

THAT NIGHT, MY MOTHER COOKED RICE and we ate and rested. We hoped that in the morning we would continue our journey to Prey Veng. To be honest, I had no idea where Prey Veng was because I had no sense of direction. All I knew was that I was a little boy there, and I remembered the house we stayed at was there.

I knew it was going to be a long journey, and this time, we hoped that my family could do it because there would not be any fighting. At that time, a lot of decisions were made based on hope and speculations. We did not get to Prey Veng.

Morning came, and we were ordered to cross the street to the other side and to continue on to a small village called Poom Am Phill Chour. There were only a few houses in this village. The rest of the space was an empty forest.

We all knew that there was nothing in Poom Am Phill Chour that could support the hundreds of people who were moving into that village. Although everyone was wondering what the Khmer Rouge were thinking, no one was brave enough to ask any questions. Or maybe they just thought it was temporary because everyone believed they would return to their houses in three days.

On the morning that we arrived, the Khmer Rouge soldiers ordered us to build a hut. They told us to cut down trees and gather palm leaves to build it. We had nothing to cut with, so the soldiers gave us a few axes and told us to share.

That was a problem because most of the people were city dwellers. They had no idea how to build anything, let alone a hut, or even where to start. My family was no exception. Even though we moved around a lot from place to place, my father never had to build his own home.

The Khmer Rouge kept on emphasizing that we would only be there for three days. Some of the families that came into this village with us did not want to build any huts because one day had passed and they thought that there were only two more days to go.

My father didn't agree with them. He did not want to wait, so he started building a hut. It was a small simple hut, but at least there was a roof over our heads protecting us from the sun. That was about it – protection from the sun.

Little did we know, it was also protection from the Khmer Rouge soldiers' rage.

The families that did not bother to build a shelter ran into trouble very soon.

On the third day, the soldiers came to each family and told us that we must come to a meeting at noon. A lot of people were confused because they were ready to go back to their houses. Some people went to the meeting and some did not.

My father went to the meeting. At the meeting, the Khmer Rouge told us that we must learn to share. Everything we owned had to be brought forward so that everyone else could use it too. Everything that the people brought from their houses now belonged to the government.

Some people did not want to give up anything, but some did. Families had to give their gold, diamonds, rice, clothes, bicycles, and whatever other possessions they had. My family did not have anything left, because we did not have anything from the beginning.

We were excused.

The next day, cooking became a shared responsibility, and everybody prepared food under one roof. We not only shared meals, but also the work. Some people had to go to find food and some people stayed and cooked.

When it was time to eat, the Khmer Rouge would signal everyone by ringing a "bell," which was actually two pieces of metal that were banged together. The soldiers assigned a few people to cook and to distribute food to all of us.

Even though this concept was new to all of us, I was kind of happy because we did not have any food left. In exchange for the food we received, all of us, young and old, had to work.

That wasn't a bad thing. In fact, I remember that I was actually enjoying it.

Most days, I went with adults to catch fish and eels further away from the village. There were a lot of snakehead or mudfish and yellow eels. The eels were slippery.

It wasn't as easy as fishing with a pole. I used an axe to hack through thick vegetation and underneath the dying and rotten vegetation, there were mudfish. We got a lot of fish that day and I had so much fun catching them that it didn't seem like work.

At first, having us fish for food seemed to be reasonable, but each day, the hours seemed to get longer. There was little rest, and every day was a working day. People, myself included, started to have different ideas. Everyone wanted to keep what they caught and share it with their family.

And all of us were tired from working.

It didn't matter that we were exhausted. My father and I went off to work every day.

His job was to clear debris in the swamp. He pulled weeds out from the swamp, removed decayed trees or tree branches, and cut through thick grass in the muddy water.

He also came across many mudfish. Some of those fish were very big. I remember seeing some that were as big as my thigh. There were also a lot of yellow eels.

By noon, everyone was allowed to rest and the food was carried to all of us by the cooks. All workers took a break for about half an hour to have lunch, and then all of us were off to work again. At first, there was plenty to eat.

But as many days passed and we continued to work, the soldiers began to ration the food.

Things were not getting better. They were getting worse, and our hopes of returning home were diminishing.

Finally, the order came down from the top that all of us were here to stay and work. It was now clear that we were not going back to the city. We weren't happy, but it did not come as a surprise. By then, most of us had expected that this depressing swamp was going to remain our home

"BUILD YOUR HUTS!" the soldiers told us. "All of the belongings must be put together to share. If anyone is caught hiding anything, that person will be punished severely."

One day at a meeting, three people asked the Khmer Rouge about returning to their homes. That night, there were the loudest screams that I ever heard in my life.

The word spread through the village so quickly that pretty much everyone was shivering. Everyone was whispering about the death of those people who had asked questions at the meeting. And their deaths were not pleasant. The story spread that they were killed and their livers were removed and eaten.

No one knew whether this was true or not, but in that rumor, there was a message to the villagers:

Do not challenge!

Everyone was frightened and, for the moment, did not know what to think anymore. Two happened. No one asked questions in the meetings, and everyone followed the directions given.

A few days later, we found out that the Khmer Rouge did kill those three individuals from my village. The screaming I heard was from those three. I'll never forget that sound or those people.

I guess the Khmer Rouge wanted to set an example and wanted people to hear their cries. It worked. They sent a clear message to all the villagers that by directly challenging them, the consequence was death. From that point on, no one dared to raise any issues with the Khmer Rouge soldiers.

My father started to build a more suitable hut. Once again, our home was only built with some wood, bamboo and palm leaves. The hut was raised about six feet above ground. There were no rooms, but just one little open space. The floor was our bed. It was made from bamboo, and at night the mosquitoes bit us through the bottom. There was no kitchen since we were not allowed to cook.

Every morning my father went off to work. My mother also worked. She carried my little brother on her back to work. My three other brothers and I also went off to work. We all worked at different places. All of the children were separated by their ages and each group would do different jobs. Some jobs were difficult and some were not. Being the oldest son in the family, I got the hardest job.

I was sent away with other children who were my age to work far away from the village. I think I was about 11 years old at that point. I remember digging the ground and carrying dirt to build a dam.

The day was long and there was hardly any food. There was no time to bathe or rest. I grew thin and weak due to the lack of food. I was tired and miserable. The only time I could rest was when it was dark outside and I could not do any work.

Even at night, before I went to sleep, I had to learn to sing the revolutionary songs. One of the songs was "Padah Nya" or "commitment to carry out orders."

Seven days a week, my father went off to work with other men in the village. He started very early in the morning and came home very late every night. His job was to plow the rice paddy.

At first, it was very difficult because my father had never done anything like this before. Even though his family in Prey Veng worked in the rice paddy, he never did. He worked in the cement factory in Kampot. He had to learn to use the plow very quickly because the Khmer Rouge were looking for students, teachers, doctors, and technicians to kill.

The Khmer Rouge believed that if they could kill all of these people, there would be no one to ask them any questions regarding their Communist rules. My father had to pretend that he was a farmer. He worked very hard just to prevent the Khmer Rouge from asking him questions.

12

All of us survived the first year with the Khmer Rouge. Early in 1976, my brothers and I were sent back to the Poom An Phill Chour for a few weeks. We still had to go to work each day, but we were allowed to sleep in our own hut with family members. That was at least a little more comfortable for us.

One day, I arrived home before my father. I saw my father from a distance as he was walking toward the house. At first, I could not tell that it was him. It was the first time that I realized that my father had lost a lot of weight. He looked so exhausted, and he walked like an eighty year old man.

As he walked, my father bent forward and he held onto a stick to support himself. Without it, I do not think he could walk. It was also the first time that I realized that my father was sick.

A year earlier, he was a healthy man. Now, he barely talked and he barely walked – but the Khmer Rouge still ordered him to work.

On one occasion, he came back from work just as I returned from work myself. My father asked me to go gather some wood to build a fire because it was getting cold. I refused to go, saying I was too tired.

My father got angry at me. He picked up a rope and twirled it together and smacked me so hard on my back that I fell down. My back was bleeding.

After he hit me, he did not say anything, but he went off to gather the wood himself. When he came back, I saw his eyes filled with tears. I think he felt sad that he hit me, but I was not angry at him.

At that point, although I was hurt physically and emotionally, I also felt very badly that my father had to get the wood himself. I knew that he had a tougher job than me, and that he must have been exhausted. But even though I wanted to help him, I really did not have the strength.

Things did not get better.

IT WAS JULY OF 1976 when my father became very ill. He worked too hard and he never had time to rest. There were no sanitation facilities and mosquitoes swarmed everywhere. Animals and humans often shared the same living space, and many people contracted malaria.

My father was one of them.

When he became ill and could not work anymore, the Khmer Rouge put him in their makeshift hospital. It was a joke.

They used children from the work fields as nurses to give injections of coconut water and gave out juice from herbal medicine. The hospital beds were made from bamboo. There were no sheets and there were no blankets. When it rained, the water often dripped onto the patients. In short, it was a slum.

Most of the people who were sick and were admitted to the hospital were often dead in three to four days. There were no medications for anyone. There was also no food.

The Khmer Rouge policy was if you could not work, you could not eat. My father could not work so he could not eat.

During the time he was in the hospital, I was able to see him once. The image of him lying on the bamboo bed, his skin stretched out, barely covering his bones, has stayed in my head forever.

Three days later, he died.

MY FATHER'S LAST WORDS, according to the patient next to him, were directed to the hospital staff. He was begging for food when he died with his eyes open.

He was only in his forties when he ended his life of suffering under this cruel regime. When he passed away, the Khmer Rouge allowed only my mother to see him. None of the children got a glimpse of him. We were all at home crying. When my mother came back home, she was still crying.

Just one year into the Khmer Rouge regime, and I had already lost a father. He survived many battles at the cement factory, but the suffering of this cruel regime ended his life. Now, my mother had to protect all of the five boys by herself.

She had to be stronger than before. My mother was alone in this village among many strangers. Most of her children were separated from her. The only child who stayed home with her was my youngest brother, Ra, who was born in 1974.

I am sure that every night she worried about her other four children working under the Khmer Rouge soldiers' supervision. I cannot imagine what went through her head. Now, as a parent with four children of my own, I understand her feelings and how hard it was for her to keep all of us alive.

WHEN MY MOTHER GOT HOME, she told us that my father's closest friend and a stranger carried my father out of the hospital to be buried. There was no coffin. They wrapped him in a mat that he slept on. There was no wake, burial ritual or anything that we know in a civilized world. During this time, Buddhist monks were disrobed and sent to work in the rice paddies.

Both men dug the ground about one foot deep, on a little hill in the middle of the rice paddy, which was just enough to cover him with dirt. That was all the burial ritual my father got.

A year later, the Khmer Rouge ordered the villagers to level the hill and use whatever was left in the ground as fertilizer. I think I was twelve years old when all of these things happened. I walked by the little hill on my way to work a few times. Whenever I looked to the hill, I said to myself that my beloved father was buried there.

Even though I was still a fairly young boy, I was mature. Even though I was sad and confused, I had to hold it in in order to survive.

My mother told all of us to be strong and pleaded with all of her children to listen to the Khmer Rouge so they would not kill us. She told us not to be lazy and not to ask them any questions. She wanted us to find inner strength so that we could survive.

I understood her at that young age.

The message from my mother to all of us was clear, and I took it in stride. However, I was worried about my younger brothers.

Did they understand what my mother was saying to them?

It didn't matter how old you were. The Khmer Rouge were very strict and the rules applied to all.

13

My family and I stayed in District Number 4 or in Khmer, *Dom Bon Boun*. It was one of the hardest hit in terms of killing and starving.

When the starvation started for the people in my village, I was not spared.

I was so skinny, I could count my ribs. My knee cap was bigger than my thigh. When I laid down, I could feel my belly touching my back spine. My pelvic hip bone stuck out sharply on both sides.

Walking and working was the hardest, because I did not have any strength to hold myself up. It was the worst human suffering I had ever experienced.

Even though it was difficult, my mother tried to take care of all of us. She was determined to keep us alive. She knew it would not be easy, and she was willing to do whatever was necessary, and that included stealing.

Once in a while, the Khmer Rouge gave us a day off because there was not any food. That didn't make sense to me.

Everyone in my village worked so hard and there was a lot of rice produced. Sometimes, there were three harvests in a year, but as soon as the harvest was done, all of the rice in the storage disappeared.

It was only during the harvest season that all of the workers got food. Everyone ate well, but as soon as rice was in storage, food rations began.

I had no idea where all the rice went.

ONE DAY MY MOTHER AND MY BROTHERS WERE HOME. I was resting in a hammock under a mango tree in front of the house. My mother was also inside resting, I believe.

When I got up, I could not see. I felt so hot all over. I yelled for my mother, and she ran out and asked me what happened. I told her that I could not see. She felt my head and my body and it was hot. She put me on her back and she ran towards the hospital.

When I arrived at the hospital, the untrained nurses told my mother that I had a fever. Until this day, I could not tell you what happened to me. I lost my eyesight. I depended on everyone around me.

My brother, Marin, pretended to be sick, so that he was sent to the hospital just to look after me. My mother came by to see me every day during work and after work. When there was a break, she ran across the rice field to see me and, at lunch break, she brought her share to me.

Marin was there to help me to the bathroom, and to protect me from other people in the hospital because I could not see. It was also my brother who fed me and made sure that other people could not steal my food. My mother could not be there to feed me because she had to go back to work

Looking back, I'm not sure if it was when I was in the hospital this time or if it was another time when I believe I was near death, but I remembered seeing a little boy, not more than two feet tall, running toward me in the hospital.

This little boy gave me a bowl of water. I was not sure what it was, but I drank that water. I did not think of anything else.

At the time, I kept it in my mind and didn't even tell my mother, who loved me and took care of me. I did not want people to think I was going crazy. If the Khmer Rouge found out that I was hallucinating, I would have been killed.

I kept the image of the little boy to myself. Little did I know that we would meet again about 20 years later.

IN THE HOSPITAL, I remember very clearly that nurses pounded some kind of leaves and mixed them with water. They placed the smashed leaves on my body to reduce the fever. They also kept pouring water on me and injecting me with coconut water.

They did not use any pills or prescriptions, like we would expect in a hospital. They used leaves and coconut water – and they used the same needle over and over.

That didn't bother me at the time. What scared me was that I was in the same situation as my father when he was in the hospital. I did not get my share of the food because I did not work.

Fortunately, my mother was not about to lose me like she lost my father. She kept her share of the food for me. She hid the food and brought it to me. This was more dangerous than it sounds. If the Khmer Rouge had caught her in the act, they would have killed her.

Even that didn't bother me. I was young and I was hungry. I did not think of anything else.

While I stayed in the hospital for many days, my mother had to beg everyone to help me.

She even went to the Khmer Rouge leader in the village to beg for food for me. I remember that the leader gave me an egg. That was the only thing I ever got from the Khmer Rouge.

The egg was good, but I do not remember anything else after that, except my mother being determined to keep me alive. While I was sick, my other brothers were out in the fields working. My mother worried about me and her other children.

I was very lucky to be alive. My mother saved my life.

My mother asked almost everyone in the village to help me. She was concerned because I could not see.

One day, she met an old man in the village and he told my mother what to do. She did not hesitate for a moment. He told her what to gather and when she was out working in the fields, she collected all of the ingredients. Little by little, she got them all.

Once she was ready, she asked the Khmer Rouge leader to let me come home. He allowed me to leave the hospital.

When I arrived home, I stayed there by myself during the day because my mother was working. In the evening, she tried to get my eyesight back. I remember that she put everything into one pot and boiled them.

After about an hour, she took the pot off the fire. She asked me to sit in front of the pot and covered me under a blanket. She told me to open up the pot cover and to release the steam into my open eyes.

I do not know what it was, but it worked. To this day, I am not sure how she met this person, but he saved my eyesight.

All of these activities were done secretly. When I was cured, and people asked me what happened, I had to say that the nurses and the medication that they used on me in the hospital worked.

Once I was cured, I went back to work.

14

I was happy to see, but I was still hungry – and the hunger seemed to get worse by the day. To survive, I had to learn to steal rice.

On many occasions, I carried my youngest brother, Ra, on my hip to help me to steal food. Sometimes, when I went to the rice field, and often when I went to the storage warehouse, I hid the rice I took between his thighs. It was not much, but it was food. When we got home, I ate the rice by myself.

My little brother and my other three brothers sat there watching me eat. I ignored them all.

My mother pleaded with me to give them some, but I just ignored her. I was like an animal.

Before the war, I was a caring and understanding young man. I helped my parents and I took care of my brothers when necessary. I loved them, but this new, cruel world of hunger, made me blind – it seemed that I had lost not only my eyesight, but also my mind. Why else would I use my little brother to steal food?

Luckily, the Khmer Rouge did not catch us. If they did, both of us would have been killed. For three years, I did this, and I never realized that it was wrong. In the years that I had lived with the Khmer Rouge, I knew nothing about what freedom was and what the rest of the world looked like. I only knew the places where I worked, the concentration camps where I lived, and the irrigation canals where I spent my time digging.

We all just thought about ourselves. Everyone was just trying to survive.

Once in a while, I would get a chance to see my brothers or my mother, but instead of being glad to see them, I turned into this ugly person. I used my brothers to get what I wanted: FOOD!

It continues to be the most horrible experience that I have had to live with. The feeling that I had for my brothers and mother during this time was unexplainable. I never could figure it out, but I have asked myself many times, how could I have done this to my own brothers and mother? I tried to convince myself that it was an illusion, but it was not. It was a real situation and my own brothers and mother were hurt from my behavior. I guess the starving and the suffering made me forget who my brothers and mother were.

The only reason that I can live with myself today is because I have convinced myself that all the things that I did to my brothers and my mother during the Communist time was because I was too young to know the difference. I was greedy and selfish.

Food was very hard to find during this time. Hatred and self-survival was probably on everyone's mind, and that included me.

Today, I am not even sure if any of my brothers remember what took place, except Marin. I am sure that I hurt them not only physically, but also emotionally, deep down inside. There was more pain and suffering than anyone could imagine. I did not know anything else during this time. If I could take back any of those times, I would, and I would correct it. The person that I am today would be willing to give his life, especially to my mother, because she protected me when I was sick

And the physical sickness was only part of the pain during this time. The regime turned friends and family members against each other. Despite the slogan and the orders, we called each other *mit* or friend, but we were anything but that.

THE KHMER ROUGE BRIBED the children to tell stories of their parents' past. They used a network of children to spy on people in their sleeping quarters and at the working fields.

As a child, you are innocent, so any information you provided was considered truthful. By starving people, especially the children, the Khmer Rouge won the battle. They could get any information from the children about their parents as long as they promised food.

Although I witnessed many of those situations during this time, I did not get any food from them because I did not have anything important to tell them. Even though I was selfish and hungry, I did not make up any stories about my mother. I guess I still had some sense of right and wrong because other children's parents were killed as soon as the children provided the information the Khmer Rouge wanted – whether it was true or not.

Although I may not have turned against my mother, I was not so protective of my brothers. I let hunger overpower me, so I did not realize that it was completely wrong.

Now, I know better. I was selfish. There was one time when hunger made me hit one of my brothers for stealing my food. I was eating by myself in the house when he came in and grabbed the rice from me.

He was also hungry, so he did not even care that I hit him. His head was bleeding, but he sat there and kept eating.

I kept on beating him on the head. Blood came out of his skull and it dripped down on his face. When I looked at him, it was like he did not even know that I hit him. The pain from the beating was nothing to him. He was too busy eating.

All these years later, I still can't get rid of the shame that I feel for letting hunger overpower love.

THROUGH ALL THE HUNGER and the suffering, I continued to work.

Some of my jobs were to collect cow manure and human waste. We then used that as fertilizer. When that was done, I cleared the bushes.

Every morning, I spread the fertilizer in the rice field. After I finished my morning job, I had to go to cut bushes and carry them back to the village. Sometimes, I had to burn the bushes and carry the ash back to the rice field. I had this job for many months.

At about the same time, my mother was working at a rice storage place. Most of the women, like my mother, had to carry their babies on their backs while working. My mother's job was to put rice into a 100 kilogram bag, or about a 220 pound bag, and sew it up.

Some men and children also worked there. The men had a different job. They carried the bags and put them away in a safe place.

Cambodian civilians bag up captured North Vietnamese rice.
In the public domain from William H. Hammond, The U.S. Army in Vietnam: The
Military and the Media, 1968-1973. Washington DC: U.S. Army Center of Military
History, 1998.

Banner of the Communist Party of Kampuchea.
Source: TheSign 1998. CC BY-SA 3.0

The Angkar

In the mid-1970s, the Communist Party of Kampuchea (CPK) referred to itself as "The Angkar." But on September 29, 1977, Pot Pol not only declared the existence of the CPK in a five-hour speech, but revealed that the supreme authority of the party rested with an obscure ruling body that had been kept in seclusion.

15

Throughout these times, the village leaders often reminded us that we belonged to the *Angkar*. I had no idea what it was, but I, at the time, thought it was the leader of the Khmer Rouge. In fact, *Angkar* was the form of government during Khmer Rouge control.

The term means, "The Organization," and for about two years prior to 1977, that was what the Communist Party of Kampuchea was known as. But whatever the name, everyone had to make a commitment to be loyal to the *Angkar*.

The Angkar was supposed to take care of us. At meetings, the leaders told us that our parents gave birth to us, but they could not own us. All of us belonged to the *Angkar*. *Angkar* owned all of the children of Cambodia, and if anyone opposed the *Angkar*, they would be eliminated.

The Khmer Rouge made it very clear to all of us. All of the children and working adults must be loyal to the *Angkar*. Anyone found lying or stealing from the *Angkar* would be punished severely. As previously mentioned, when people asked the Khmer Rouge about returning to the city, they were all killed, so there were many examples already how the Khmer Rouge executed people.

Their tactics worked. We were all afraid.

IN 1977, THE SITUATION BECAME WORSE. Once again, all of the children were separated from their families. My three brothers and I were taken away by the Khmer Rouge and then we were split up according to ages. Each group was sent off to work at a different location. Some were far away from the village and some were close by. Once every five to six months, we were allowed to come home to see our parents for a few hours.

I was sent far away from the village. I do not know where, but I know that it took about half a day to get there. I was too young to remember the exact location. When I was there, I remembered that I got up very early in the morning and went off with about thirty children to work.

During the day, we had a few fifteen minute breaks. We did not have much food to eat and we came back to the camp very late every day. The children's jobs ranged from cutting bushes to gathering manure. One of the hardest jobs was trying to build a dam in the moving water with a hoe.

It was an impossible job, but we had to do it.

The water was deep, and in some places, the water was up to our necks. I was at this job for about eight months. Sometimes, I wondered how we were going to do it, but no one dared to ask any questions. All of us just followed the Khmer Rouge directions. It was a silly task, but everyone had to stay in the water from before sunrise until the sun had set.

Every morning at around four o'clock, the Khmer Rouge soldiers blew a whistle to wake up us up to go to work. At that time of day, most of the soldiers were not even awake yet. They just blew the whistle and then they went back to sleep in their hammocks.

Once we heard the whistle blow, we had to get up and stand in a straight line and be ready to go. About ten minutes later, the soldiers got up to inspect us.

The soldiers walked around and made sure that we were in a straight line, awake and ready to work. If we were out of line, we would get whipped and yelled at.

All of us were just little boys who were separated from our families. We were scared and hungry – and we followed the soldiers' directions or risked getting whipped.

When we worked in the water, we had leeches sucking blood everywhere on our legs. For me, that was the first time I had this creature attached to my legs.

When I first saw a leech, I ran. But the leeches would not fall off. I was so scared and I did not know what to do. At first I asked other kids to help me take them off my legs.

Soon, there were so many of them attached to my legs, I had to be brave. I had to take them off myself. When I pulled them off, there seemed to be two sucking ends to the leeches.

As I walked in the filthy water, which was full of leeches, I felt certain parts of my legs were tight. Those were the leeches attaching themselves to me.

When I lifted my legs up, that's when I saw leeches on them. I pulled them off, and threw them away. But we were still in the same water and in a few minutes, there were more.

It seemed that those leeches liked the same spot on my legs. They just kept attaching themselves and all these years later, I still have a few of those scars.

I was so tired, but I kept pushing myself to do what I was told. Sometimes I felt very sad because I missed my brothers and my mother. But most of the time, I was just hungry and exhausted.

AT THE WORK CAMP, I never had a good night's sleep or enough food to eat. I slept on a hill surrounded by water. The mosquitoes were unbearable. The food was even worse.

Dirt was my bed, the clothes I wore were my blanket, and the sky was my roof. Next to me were animals, including domestic cows and water buffalos that were used to work in the fields. The place was to be damp and muddy all the time because people and animals shared the same space.

But still I had to push myself to work; otherwise, the Khmer Rouge would have killed me. For three and a half years under the Khmer Rouge control I never once had anything good to eat. Lunch was always a cupful of water with a little rice in it. All we had was salt to add flavor to the rice. For dinner, it was the same thing as lunch. Day after day, we ate the same thing: plain rice and, if we were lucky, a little salt.

By this time, I was so skinny. As a growing 11 or 12 year old boy, I needed food. So I learned to survive.

Every time I was at work and standing in the water, I tried to catch crabs, frogs, fish, snails or anything that floated around me. If we got caught, we would be in trouble, so I looked left and then I looked right. Quickly I grabbed whatever swam by and put it in my mouth as quickly as possible so the Khmer Rouge could not see me.

Everyone was doing it because we were hungry. If we brought anything back to the camp, we had to share it with the group with our *mit,* our friends. I was not going to do that. I needed some strength, and the only way that I could have it was to eat all that I could find.

In order to survive, I had to hide and try to eat my catch without being seen. Many times, the crab claws pinched my tongue because I was not quick enough. Despite the pain, this found food was delicious.

After a while, the Khmer Rouge realized that trying to build the dam was impossible. They decided that we should be moved to another job. So we moved.

WE MIGHT HAVE CHANGED LOCATIONS, but the new job assigned by the Khmer Rouge was not much different from the old job. Every morning, we had to wake up at about four o'clock to the Khmer Rouge soldier who still blew the whistle.

Once we heard the whistle blow, we had to form a single line. This time, we had to go into the water and cut weeds. My job was to pull weeds from one place and put them in another place.

Then the water would move them back again, and I had to pull them back up again. It was the same thing, day in and day out. It made no sense, but I still had to do it.

No one dared to ask questions. Even though we knew that the job was silly, we continued to pull the weeds, put them in another place, and pull them back up again when the water moved them.

No one asked questions.

We knew for a fact that, if we dared ask anything, we would be killed. Killing seemed to be a favorite activity for the Khmer Rouge.

The water was very dirty and full of leeches. During the flooding season, the land eroded. The dead grasses and the dead tree branches, as well as different kinds of insects, would come up to the surface. It even changed the color of the water from clear to milk chocolate brown. The water colors changed, but the job didn't.

We worked pulling weeds in this dirty water from before sunrise until sunset. The only time we stopped for a break was to eat a bowl of rice soup, and then we had to go down to work again. Another break was for dinner, and that was another bowl of rice soup.

Day after day, we had to do these nonsense activities.

When I returned to the camp each night I was there alone. My brothers were somewhere else and my mother was at the village.

Camp was in the middle of nowhere. I had no idea where I was and I still cannot recall any directions to that place. I think I was on this job with other children for about six months, but I know that I did not come back to the village until late in 1978.

16

Every day the Khmer Rouge leaders brought children from different villages to work at our camp or at one of the other two that were nearby. The children were usually the ones who stole food. They were placed in these camps as punishment. But, according to the government, they were at these camps to be re-educated.

During that time, I heard from several different people that one of my brothers, Marith, had been captured by the Khmer Rouge. One day he did not go to work, but he went fishing for frogs in a pond. The Khmer Rouge leader saw him and made sure that he was punished.

Every night I waited to see him. All of the children that the Khmer Rouge brought to the concentration camps, or "re-education camps," had to pass by my camp, which was the first of the three camps.

The information I had received was correct.

My brother had been caught and they were going to kill him, but they were not going to send him to the concentration camp. They sentenced him to death because he was not working.

They wanted to kill him to send a message to the whole village that anyone who avoided work would be punished. Looking back, I cannot think of anything that made me feel worse. There were so many things that went through my head.

He was just a little boy who was hungry. It was not his fault.

If I could, I would have given my life for his but, not knowing what else to do, I turned to the spiritual world.

"Lord Buddha," I prayed, "Take care of him and to spare his life."

Before they sent him away, however, they brought him to the village and tied him to a pole in the area where we ate for everyone to see. My mother was there and she saw her own son tied to the pole.

He was crying because he did not know what had happened. My mother was crying, but was not allowed to comfort him.

The Khmer Rouge did not give him any food, and he had to watch everyone else eating. Once they finished this torture and tormented him, they sent him off to be killed.

My mother was crying. I was not there and none of my other brothers were there. My mother was there with my youngest brother to witness this horrid act. I could only imagine the pain that my mother endured at this time.

She went through so much in her life. At this junction, she had to witness her own son tied to a pole and she was helpless, powerless and hopeless.

NO ONE IN MY FAMILY KNEW where the Khmer Rouge sent my brother. All my family knew was that he was going to die. They sent him off with an old man who was supposed to kill him.

They left our village.

My mother was sobbing because she thought for sure that she had seen the last of her own son. She had not.

The old man traded his life and let my brother live.

Maybe my prayer to Lord Buddha was answered or maybe the spiritual world heard my cry, but all I know is that my brother came home and the old man was killed.

My brother told my mother that he slept in a house somewhere for two days. On the third day, he was sent out to be killed. If it were not for the old man's kindness and self-sacrifice, he would have been dead.

My mother, once again, tried to keep him home and out of sight.

17

Food was scarce. About twelve ounces of rice for one hundred people was one day's ration.

People who went to work fell down in the rice field from hunger and exhaustion. Many times my mother and I collapsed because we were just so tired. The hours were long, and people died all around us.

During this time, if anyone had found one grain of rice sticking to a dog's tail, people would have killed each other for it. There was a saying in Cambodia:

"There are houses, but no one lives in them; there are roads, but no one walks on them."

This was so true during the Communist regime in Cambodia.

When food became so scarce, the Khmer Rouge let people come home to be with their family. Those were the joyful moments because even though we had nothing, at least we were together.

When I returned to the village, I stayed up at night trying to hit mice or rats that ran around the hut. In the darkness, I stayed still in one place, and held a stick in my hand waiting to hit whatever ran in front of me. Sometimes I caught a few mice and that would be a lucky night.

Whenever I caught a mouse, even in the middle of the night, I built a small fire and cooked the mouse no matter what time it was.

After burning it, I took the mouse out of the fire and scraped it with a stick and then burned it again. When it looked like it was cooked, I ate it right there.

I ate rats, mice, leaves, crabs, snails, snakes – in short, anything that could be eaten. At the time, I didn't think about sanitation, and I didn't care if it was gross or uneatable, or even if there were germs or bacteria. I didn't care where those creepy crawling things had been. It was about survival.

DESPITE EATING WHATEVER I COULD catch, my body became swollen like a balloon. The skin on my body, legs and arms stretched to the limit. My body was full of water. Sometimes, the skin cracked and water dripped out, just like tears that flowed from my eyes.

My mother could not stand seeing all of us starving, so one day, she left all of us at home and went off to search for food very early in the morning. She told us to be quiet and stay in the house.

She went off with another woman in the village to look for any kind of fruit. She told me to tell the leader of the village that she was very sick if they were looking for her.

All of us were so worried because we did not know where she had gone and what she would steal or where she would steal it. Our biggest concern was that she would get caught and the Khmer Rouge would kill her.

There were a lot of thoughts that went through my head and my brothers' heads. We talked about it, but not in great detail. I remembered some of the concerns we had were what would happen if they killed our mother? What would we do?

The short answer was, we did not know what to do.

I looked at my brothers and we were all sad. We did not have to say anything to each other. We knew for a fact that if she did not come back, the Khmer Rouge had caught her.

We went to eat in the cafeteria as usual, and after we ate, we came back home. We did not talk to anybody.

My brothers and I pretended that nothing had happened in our household. We were sad and we kept waiting for her return. We waited at the hut for a long time and later that night she came back.

She came back with oranges and each of us got four.

We were so happy. It was the first time that we had had oranges in three years. They were delicious.

After this one ordeal, she never went back to steal those oranges again, because she was afraid that if they caught her in the act, they would kill her and all of her children would be orphans.

She did not want to take that chance again.

SOON THERE WAS A NEW ORDER from the Khmer Rouge leader. Everyone, young and old, must work digging up a pond. We must work day and night.

At first, we did not know why and no one dared to ask. It was still 1978, and the starving was unbearable. Just a half-pound of rice – one eight-ounce can of rice – now fed one hundred people.

Even though we were starving, we knew that there was plenty of rice being produced. But they would not feed us.

Each night, we heard the sound of trucks coming into the village to load up the rice. By morning, the storage was almost empty.

It was as if the Khmer Rouge expected something to happen.

My brother Marin and I did not go back to camp. We stayed in the village, hiding from the Khmer Rouge leaders.

It did not work.

The Khmer Rouge came to the village to look for us. They went to our house and they asked my mother. She told them that my brother and I had left the village and gone back to the camp.

Actually, we were hiding behind the bamboo bushes. We climbed up a tree and hid there for half a day.

Luckily, they did not catch us. It was a good thing. If they had caught us then, we would definitely have been killed.

One can call it fate or just pure luck, but either way the timing was great.

During the time when the Khmer Rouge regime was in charge, there were no communication devices allowed. No radio, television, school or anything else. Despite this, rumors spread, and somehow people got information.

We learned that every province in Cambodia was empty. Factories were shut down. Money and books were burned for heat and fuel.

The cities and towns were empty. Every citizen worked in the countryside – and everyone was eager to get back to their homes after many years passed.

A FEW DAYS LATER, we heard that the Vietnamese forces were coming; everyone in the village stopped working. Some of the Khmer Rouge leaders ran away and others stayed behind and tried to get us to work.

My mother did not go to work.

My three other brothers were with my mom at home. At the time my brother, Marin and I were still hiding from the Khmer Rouge.

We later learned that the pond that the Khmer Rouge had forced the people to work so hard on was to bury all of the people in the village. That was the plan. Mass extermination.

Thank goodness, they did not succeed.

Army of the Republic of Vietnam (ARVN) on a road in Cambodia.
Photo by U.S. Department of Defense in the public domain.

18

We waited for the Vietnamese forces to come to rescue us for many days and we did not see them. We started to wonder if we were ever going to be rescued at all.

Early one morning, when we got up and we were preparing to go to work, the whole village was quiet. No one seemed to go out of their huts.

Later that day, in the late afternoon, we learned that all of the leaders in the village had left except for one.

We were a little bit confused, and no one seemed to know what to do.

With nothing to do, I went to a pond about half a mile from the village to try to catch fish. The pond water was milky, but there were fish in there.

About ten people were already in the pond catching fish with their bare hands. I went down to join them.

Just as I was getting started, I saw a Khmer Rouge soldier pointing his AK-47 at me from the top of the pond. He kept screaming at me and the rest of the people in the pond to get out.

I thought I was going to die. I was so scared.

For just a few minutes, the soldier stood there, ordering all of us at gun point to get out of the pond. Then he ran off.

Although I did not know what happened, I tried to get out of the pond as quickly as I could and started to run toward the village.

When I got back to the village, I saw that a group of people had gone into the rice storage area and had taken the rice to their huts. Apparently, the Khmer Rouge soldiers and all of the leaders had left the village for good.

I was so happy. I did not have to go to work anymore.

The people in the village, including my family, stayed in the village for two more days, because we did not know what to do. Some people got themselves ready to go back into the city, and some others went off looking for revenge.

My family and I stayed put in our hut.

THAT NIGHT, TANKS ROLLED into Battambang province. The tanks traveled on the main road, which was close enough to the village.

We heard a lot of loud noises. My mother woke us up and we ran to the rice field, even though we did not know was happening. We thought it was going to be another shooting.

When the noise stopped, we went back to the hut.

There was not any more fighting or any resistance from the Khmer Rouge soldiers. Thank goodness, there was not, because we were so tired.

By word of mouth we learned that the Vietnamese force occupied the city and we should leave the village. The next morning, we saw people heading toward Battambang. People in my village ran across the rice field toward the main street which led to the city.

My mother hesitated for a moment. She was unsure of the whole situation. I think we were the last family to get out of the village.

When we got to the main street, we saw a lot of people. It was just like the time we left the city three years earlier. This time, however, it was different because all of us wore black clothes and all of us looked skinny. None of the people were on bicycles or carried any belongings with them.

We had to sleep on the road for one night before we made our way into the city. That night was the first time in years that we were able to cook our own food. It was kind of scary. We did not see any soldiers; neither the Khmer Rouge nor the Vietnamese were around.

We quickly moved into the city. Finally, we were free.

19

There was nothing that compared to the happiness and joy we felt in our hearts that day. To say the least, it was a big relief. But life didn't get easier.

Our suffering under the Khmer Rouge was over, but when we got to the city, we could not find our house. It had been destroyed and tall grass had replaced it. We lived on the streets of Battambang for many months.

Once again, we did not have much food. My mother was able to steal some rice from the village where we used to live. While in Battambang, we searched for our relatives. My mother found one of her brothers. He had lost his wife, but he still had his five children left.

At that time, hundreds of people were leaving the city and heading for Thailand. My mother and her brother decided that we should all go with them. While we were preparing ourselves to go, accidents kept on happening.

My uncle built a cart to carry our pots and pans, a small sack of rice, and the few change of clothes that we were able to collect when we came into the city. The cart kept breaking down. As if that wasn't bad enough, we kept on getting sick.

We never did make it out of Battambang. For four to five days we tried to get out of the city, but by then, the people who went before us came back. The Thai government had dropped off all the people at the Dangrek Mountain. From what I heard, it was a dangerous place. The people who came back to the city told horrible stories. Many people had died because there was not any water, and there were a lot of land mines along the way which exploded, killing and injuring many.

My mother and uncle thanked Buddha for stopping our journey.

WE DECIDED TO STAY in Battambang. My uncle built a house on one of the lots and we moved in with his family. Since there were so many people in both of our families, some of us had to sleep outside of the house. I slept outside with a few of my cousins and my brothers. We stayed with him for about a month. Then we left them.

We crossed the Stung Sangkae River to the other side and lived in someone's yard in a housing project that was still standing. It was not the factory housing project where we had lived, but it was similar.

My mother was able to find people to help her build an addition on the project, and then a small hut. It was a small place, but it covered our heads when it rained. We were sheltered, but we soon ran out of food. I decided that it was time to venture off to find food.

One day, I went with a group of nearby people to look for food. These people had an ox and an ox cart. I left the house in the morning with four adults. They let me tag along because they felt sorry for my family – or maybe they had another motive. I was too young to know the difference. I was just happy that they let me go with them.

We went off into dangerous areas to find rice. We were gone for at least four days. It was not planned that way, but we could not find any food along the way. We went from village to village and the rice storage we came across was empty. Other people had gotten there ahead of us.

We kept on going further and further into the unknown. We went from one empty village to the next in search for food. The villages that we came across had no one living in them. We crossed many rice fields. We crossed muddy waters and passed through many empty dry areas in search of food.

Finally, we came to one really remote place. There were several houses in this village. There were a few trees and a lot of banana trees.

And there was one rice storage area that had not been touched by anyone.

We were the first ones there, but the danger was not over yet. Many people whom we met along the way told us that the Khmer Rouge had planted grenades inside most of the storage areas. All of the people that we came across told us the same thing. Who knew if it was real or not, but that was the message that passed along.

When we saw this rice storage area untouched by people, I was happy, but at the same time, I remembered what other people were saying along the way. I was very nervous, and I was exhausted from the long trip. The three adults that I went with told me to get in there. I did what I was told – but I was very scared. I went in and I was very careful when shoveling the rice into the bags.

Nothing exploded. We came out of that place with ten bags of rice. Each bag of rice weighed about one hundred kilograms, or about two hundred twenty pounds. They were so heavy.

When we were loading the rice onto the cart, we noticed that there was fighting not too far from us between the Vietnamese force and the Khmer Rouge. We heard gun shots and we saw a lot of smoke.

We hurried out of that place and fast.

THE OXEN WERE ALMOST AS SKINNY as we were. They were tired and hungry, and so were we. But we kept on traveling and did not even stop long enough for the oxen to rest or to eat.

Coming out of that village, we traveled the same way as we entered. We met many of the same people and we told them that there was rice in the village ahead.

The rice field was muddy and water was everywhere. Our oxen were so tired that they could not pull the carts through the wet muck.

There were four of us making the trek. All of the adults whom I went with had gotten off – except one who had to help steer the cart.

They told me to get behind one of the ox and to hit it so it would go forward. Being young, I was about 14 years old at the time, I did not know any better, so I did what I was told.

At first, nothing happened, so I kept on hitting the ox. The ox laid down in the muddy water. So I kept on hitting harder and harder. The ox got up, but when it did, it kicked me.

The right rear leg of the ox hit my thigh and I flew up in the air and fell down in the muddy water. When I got up, I could barely walk. When I rolled up my pants to see the damage, I saw the perfect shape of the ox's hoof. It was painful.

The adults decided that there was too much weight for the oxen to handle, so they had to get rid of some of the rice. I think they dumped three bags. Now, the oxen could pull the cart a little better.

Two adults and I walked behind the cart. After traveling about six or seven miles from the village where we had gotten the rice, we stopped to rest in an open area.

It was not a village, and so there were no houses around. We saw one big open space, with a roof over it, so we went there. There were no walls, but it was quiet.

We were exhausted and the oxen were too, and so we decided to rest for just one night. There were no candles, so there was no light. It was very dark and it was very quiet. The only sound was from the crickets.

Every one of us was scared stiff, but tired enough to sleep. I slept on the rice that was on the cart. The adults slept at the bottom of the cart, but inside the covered area. We were still very scared of the Khmer Rouge, and also worried that people who could not find rice for food might come to kill us.

I did not sleep very well that night. Neither could anyone else.

IT WAS STILL DARK, but it was morning when we left that place. We traveled for many hours before we saw sunlight. When we reached the main road, it was almost dark again.

We kept on going until we could not go anymore. We ended up resting one more time.

This time, it was not so bad. We stayed on the main road and it was near the Battambang city. I was able to sleep for a few hours. There were also other people who rested on the main road with us.

Early that morning, we packed up again and went into the city. When we reached the patrol gate, just before the entrance into the city, we met a group of soldiers. They wanted some rice from us otherwise they would not let us in.

We ended up giving them a bag and a half. It came to about one hundred and fifty kilograms or enough to feed ten people for a couple months.

On the fourth day, the sun was just rising but the sky was still dark when I got back to the house. I saw my mother sitting there crying. She had been crying for two days. She thought that I was dead.

People had told my mother that they saw our group go behind the fighting line and that we were probably dead. She did not sleep nor eat. She did not have any food anyway.

The people that I went with gave me a bag of rice. From that moment on, my mother did not let me go to search for food anymore.

20

One day, my mother and I went off to look for firewood in the nearby villages and towns near the city. It was not easy. We did not want to go very far. Sometimes we were lucky, and we found a few buried poles in the ground. We dug them up with a hoe. Sometimes it took us all day to dig up one pole because it was buried so deep.

Once we found the poles, we took them home and chopped them up. If we had more than enough wood for us, we would try to sell the extras. Usually, we traded the firewood for rice at the market, but the rice that we received from the trade could not support the six of us for very long. The supply of rice that we had from my four day trip to search for food did not last very long.

We were lucky to have wood to trade from time to time. There was no currency in 1979. People bartered for goods, but we didn't have enough for ourselves let alone extra to exchange.

To make the situation even worse, my youngest brother Ra had the measles. There was medication in the market, but we did not have any rice, gold or silver to trade. He was so sick.

We sat there watching him die.

There was nothing we could do. All we could do was cry.

My brother slept helplessly and without hope. His stomach shrunk until it touched his backbone. We could count his ribs. The only thing we saw on him were bones and the skin that held him together. It brought back the memories that we had during the Khmer Rouge regime when we all looked like that.

Our neighbors told us to try different things. Some told us to get earth worms, put them in coconut water, and have him drink only the juice. We tried whatever the people told us, because we were desperate. I think sickness was one cause of his suffering, but not enough food and poor nutrition were also part of the problem. Somehow, Ra came out of it.

WE MOVED BACK to live with my uncle, who lived in Battambang, hoping that we could find some way to get food to feed all of us. While we stayed with him, we made waffles to sell on the street. That did not work out.

We left him again and went back to live in our old area, which was also in Battambang. This time people who lived near us felt sorry for my family, and they helped build a small house that attached to the yard of the housing project.

I decided to go to the Thai and Khmer border to search for food. I did not know what I was doing. I did not have any gold to trade. People that I went with had gold and they traded for merchandise to bring back to the city to sell. I just went along to learn.

It was a long journey, but I made three trips to the border. Because I did not know where I was going, I walked in the jungle with a group of other people. When they said, "run," I ran. When they said, "stop," I stopped.

I did not have any food or water, and so I ended up drinking my own urine. If I was lucky enough, I found milky water that was left behind from the rain. If I found any water at all, it was in people's foot prints. Most of the time, the water looked like coffee milk.

Finally, when we arrived at the border, there was plenty of water. It was in the rice field that the Thai villagers planted. We found bushes to sleep under near the Cambodian border and waited for the Thai people to bring goods to sell. Usually, it was a quick trade, because they did not want the Thai soldiers to see them.

AT THE BORDER there were no houses, just trees. Sometimes we stayed under the trees and waited for the Thai merchants to cross the border to sell their products. Once the buyers got the products they wanted, they returned to the city of Battambang. The prices on the products usually were double or triple the original prices. After watching the others, I learned how the system worked. On the third trip, I bought some things to trade.

My mother borrowed a small amount of gold from one of the neighbors for me to go buy the products from the border. I think the gold was about one-fourth of an ounce. My plan was to go to the Cambodian-Thai border to buy sugar. I was successful.

I was part of a group of about forty people who were returning to the city after our trading mission. Along the way back, we met a group of six to seven soldiers. They stopped us.

It was night. I could not see what army they were with, but they wanted to take all of our merchandise. We ended up giving it to them and I went home empty-handed. It was my last trading mission. Soon after, my family decided to leave Cambodia.

The Thai Border

For decades, there has been war in Cambodia. During the Indochina Wars in the 1970s, South Vietnamese troops supported by the United States fought North Vietnamese soldiers in Cambodia, while Communist guerrillas, known as the Khmer Rouge, battled against government soldiers. In 1975, the Khmer Rouge succeeded in their grab for power and ruled the country with terrible brutality until 1978, when the Vietnamese invaded Cambodia and installed a new government. However, Khmer Rouge remnants, other guerrilla groups and Cambodian government forces continued to fight each other until a peace treaty was signed in 1991. Each new about of fighting caused tens of thousands of Cambodians to flee their country to seek safety in Thailand.

21

When my youngest brother was well enough to walk, my family decided to leave Battambang province and headed for Thailand. One very early morning in 1979, we left the house, crossed the Sanker River by canoe, and took off on foot with another family that lived in the same housing project.

We left early in the morning because we did not want anyone to know that we were making the journey to the border. In fact, my family still owed these nice people the gold that we borrowed. In order for us to get to the border of Thailand and Cambodia, we had to make our journey from Battambang province to the Svay or Sisophon, a small town in northwestern Cambodia.

It was a difficult trip, because most of the roads were blocked off by soldiers stationed there to prevent people from leaving the city. One of the many reasons that we left Cambodia was because we were once again starving. We knew that if we stayed in Cambodia we would die, but if we went to the Thai-Cambodia border we had a good chance of surviving. Our attitude at that time was that if we were going to die, at least we would die together.

So we took the chance knowing that our journey was risky.

When we arrived at the first place that was blocked off by soldiers, we were hesitant. We did not know what was going to happen to us. Would they let us pass? Arrest us? Or worse? We had no idea what to do, so we stopped and watched the others who were in front of us.

To our surprise, we saw people crossing past the guards. Nothing happened to them, so my mother decided to take the chance.

One by one, we crossed the checkpoint. We told the soldiers that our relatives lived in the town ahead. They hesitated at first, then they decided to let us go.

When we came to the next stop, we used the same excuse. And then, it worked on the third checkpoint. We were beginning to feel more optimistic, but that wouldn't last long.

Our final stop in Cambodia was at one of the villages along the road to Sisaphon, also known as *Svay* and *Serei Saophoan*. This city is the provincial capital of Banteay Meanchey, Cambodia. If we made it through this check point, we would make it to the Thai border.

At this last stop, the soldiers stopped everyone from going in. We were stuck there for many hours. Eventually, we decided not to go through the checkpoint. Our only hope was to find an alternate route to freedom.

LATER THAT SAME AFTERNOON, we paid people to bring us across the Serei Sophorn, a medium-sized river, to the other side. I think we gave them some of the rice that was supposed to be our food for our journey.

When we were on the other side of the river, we hid and crawled from bush to bush to escape the eyes of the soldiers. At one point, they saw us and they shot at us, but we were able to get away.

When we arrived in Sisophon, it was dark. We wanted to go on, but we could not because the Vietnamese soldiers were guarding the exit. This was the Vietnamese frontline and the soldiers were protecting the town from the Khmer Rouge.

If we made it through Sisophon, we would be in Thailand. At first, we were afraid, but after a while, the fear was gone. There were a lot of things going through our heads – the possibility of death was one. But there was no time for fear, and we really had nothing to lose. At one point, my mother said to all of us, "We rather die quickly than to prolong our suffering."

And so we continued our walk to freedom.

We stayed about 200 yards from the soldiers, who told us not to go any further because the Khmer Rouge were on the other side. We told the soldiers that we would not attempt to go. We were just passing by.

We lied.

None of my family members slept that night. Thank God that my little brother did not cry. We kept our eyes on the soldiers. When they switched guards, we ran across the line into the unknown. It was scary, but we kept on running. We did not stop until we got far away from the soldiers. We walked in the darkness for many hours.

Although we didn't know where we were, we were pretty sure we were closer to escaping the pain and suffering that plagued us for years. And so we walked on.

IT WAS ALMOST DAYLIGHT when we ran into a group of about twenty people. After escaping from the soldiers and walking through mud and water for most of the night, we found ourselves in danger again. There was a robbery in progress right in front of us.

The thieves told us to stop, but we ran into the grassy field. Luckily, they could not see us and we were safe from them. We did not know who was robbing the people. They could have been Thai or Cambodian soldiers.

Most of us did not have any shoes or even flip-flops on. When we ran across the field, it was so painful because of the pointy grass blades. They ripped our feet because we did not have any protection. My little brother was about five years old, so my mother carried him on her back. After running for a while, my mother told all of us to lie down in the tall grass. All of us did and we hid until darkness fell.

That night there were a lot of mosquitoes. They bit us so much, but we did not dare to make a noise. The robbers were still not far from us, and we could hear them talking.

We stayed very quiet. None of my brothers were crying, which was good because if anyone of us had made any noise at all, we could all have been killed. There was another group next to us and they kept telling us not to give our position away to the robbers and to make sure that we kept all the children quiet. Who knows what they would have done to us if my brothers were to cry

When the sun came up, we emerged from the tall grass and went forward. We kept on walking without knowing in which direction we were heading. All we knew was that we were going forward to the Thai border.

We walked all day until we came to a small village in the middle of nowhere with about five houses. We could not figure out how these houses got there, but there were a lot of people there. I assumed that everyone in this small town was heading to the Thailand border and we were right.

Late in the afternoon, we saw a group of people leaving the village, so we followed them out. We walked until sunset. Along the way, we did not see any water nor did we have any food, but we did see many dangerous traps that were made from bamboo, landmines and dead bodies. These were the same kind of bamboo traps that my mother was making when we were in Kampot.

IT WAS A DANGEROUS JOURNEY. Fortunately, we could tell if there were landmines or traps because someone who went before us had put a stick up and made a circle. It was a danger sign for those who followed. We avoided those spots. In some places, we had to step in the footsteps of people walking in front of us.

When we got closer to the border, we ran into the Khmer Freedom Fighters who were hiding behind the trees. Usually, soldiers would make us afraid, but in this case, we were very happy because we knew that we were near the border.

When we got to the border, it was dark. We had to cross one last big pond to get to the other side. When we finally arrived, there were hundreds of other people waiting to get into the camp near the border.

The Sisophon River.
Photo released into the public domain in 2007 by Kiensvay

22

The Khmer Freedom Fighters did not allow us to get into their camp. They told us to sleep outside the camp that night. The soldiers came by carrying their AK-47 and M-16 rifles and ordered us not to build any fires or turn on flashlights or any kinds of lights. They wanted total darkness and everyone needed to be quiet. They also warned us that the Vietnamese could shell us at any time.

"Be careful!" they said. We were so close, but clearly not out of danger yet.

My family slept together in one place. My mother told all of us to sleep along a shallow strip of land that someone had dug. She told us that if the Vietnamese or the Khmer Rouge shelled us, and if we died, at least we would be buried. And so, we slept in one straight row in our possible grave, but none of us made a sound.

Once again, we were in a strange area, not knowing what would happen to us. We did know that we could die anytime from any combination of Vietnamese, Khmer Rouge, Khmer Freedom Fighter soldiers or even from the hundreds of people who shared the same space with us. It was a lawless area and nobody knew who these soldiers were. Even the people who we were with were all strangers, and no one knew their exact motives.

DESPITE THESE DANGERS and concerns, for a moment, I felt happy because now I knew we were very close to the Thai border, but then in the next moment, I felt scared. I was afraid that if the Vietnamese shelled the border, the bombs would hit my family. Luckily, nothing happened that night.

Early the next morning, the gate opened and the Khmer Freedom Fighters let us into a holding camp near the border. We were searched by the soldiers before they allowed us to get in. The name of this camp was *Chum Rom Chas*, which means "the old camp." We stayed at this camp for two days. The soldiers passed out rice. My family received five cups of rice which was more than we had in a long time.

Things were looking better.

We left "the old camp" and went to *Chum Rom Thmay*, which means "the new camp." This camp was about half a day's walk from the other camp. We stayed at "the new camp" for about three months.

Chum Rom Thmay was in the middle of nowhere. It was surrounded by forests, rice paddies. There was also a Thai village whose name I didn't know across from us, which we looked upon every day. There were no jobs, and little food or clean water to drink. Bathroom facilities were wherever you found a private area, near the bush or behind the tree.

Even though water and food was being shipped in by the United Nations Higher Commission for Refugees (UNHCR), there was no guarantee we would get any. Sometimes water and food came and sometimes it did not.

When food and water arrived, it was given to the head of the camp and somehow, most of the food ended up in the black market. Some families had gold, and they used it to exchange for goods. But my family did not have anything to trade. So we usually received nothing.

Some people dug wells to get water and some went to a nearby Thai village to get water. There were people scattered all around in one area, living and sleeping under anything they could find. It was like cows in the fields, except these were human beings.

We still suffered, but as bad as it was, things were better. We were free from torture, forced labor and execution, but we were not free from hunger. We also saw the ugly side of human beings when it came to greed.

Food and water was supposed to be shared among campers, but often, the people that were supposed to be in charge, did very little to ensure that we received our share. My family slept under a tree for about two months and we did not have any blankets or mats to sleep on. People passed by us, without acknowledging us, and never offered to help.

Here I was, with my mother and four younger brothers, sleeping under the tree for months, going unnoticed by anyone. It was like we were invisible.

I was a just a kid, probably about 15 years old, and my brothers were even younger. None of us, including my mother, had any idea of how to build a shelter.

Every night, we curled our feet and put our hands together. For many damp nights, dirt was our floor, leaves were our roof, and the clothes on our backs were our blankets. We had no home.

Although we did not have enough food to eat, at least we were not starving. Sometimes we had rice soup and sometimes we just had rice. The most difficult part of it was that we did not have anything to eat with the rice. There was no beef, pork, chicken or vegetables to go with it.

At least we weren't starving anymore. The good thing is that we did not have to go look for food. We received rice and sometimes dry salty fish that was distributed through the UNHCR.

It looked like we were going to be staying here for a while. It was time to try to find some shelter.

AFTER A COUPLE OF MONTHS, I started to look at other people's huts and tried to imagine how they were made. One day, I tried to build a hut, but it kept on falling down because I did not know what I was doing.

Finally, I got the frame to stay up, using four poles. I tied a branch from one pole to the next, and then I used small tree branches for the roof. My hut was about three feet above the ground, and it was square – kind of. If I could take a picture of it and show you right now, you would probably laugh so hard. It was the most despicable hut I ever saw, but it was home.

The grass below the rough shelter was our bed. We crawled into it to sleep every night, because it was not tall enough for us to stand. If it was too hot outside, we would crawl in to sit in the shade.

It was better than nothing, but its location was far from ideal. There were no bathroom facilities, and after spending a few months under the tree, the only place left to build was near the bush where people went to relieve themselves. When it was hot, it smelled awful.

At least we were relatively safe, but still not out of danger.

People went into the Thai village to buy food and merchandise to sell at the camp. Many times they got killed by the Thai Rangers. I came close to death myself.

Once I went to buy a block of ice from the Thai village to sell at the camp, but I ended up being chased and fired at by the Thai Rangers. I dropped the ice and ran back across the rice paddy to the camp.

The Khmer Freedom Fighters rushed out from the camp and opened fire. Here I was, caught in the middle of a gun fight again.

I never seemed to have any luck whenever I tried to do something. My body shook with fear. From that point on, I never went back again.

We ate whatever the UNHCR provided to us. If we got food, we ate – and if we did not get any, we did not eat. Sometimes we went for days without bathing because water was very precious.

One day, the UNHCR asked all the people in the camp to come into Thailand. Many people were ready to leave, including my family, but the soldiers blocked us from leaving.

"If we leave our country, who will be staying behind. We must be loyal to our land. We must be committed to our land," the soldiers said to us.

Khao I Dang – Refugee camp in 1980 (left to right)
Tha Chhun, Ra Men, Makna Men, Marin Men, Marith Men,and Ka Men

United Nations High Commission for Refugees

The Office of the United Nations High Commissioner for Refugees (UNHCR) was established on Dec. 14, 1950 by the United Nations General Assembly. The agency is mandated to lead and co-ordinate international action to protect refugees and resolve refugee problems worldwide. Its primary purpose is to safeguard the rights and well-being of refugees. It strives to ensure that everyone can exercise the right to seek asylum and find safe refuge in another State, with the option to return home voluntarily, integrate locally or to resettle in a third country. It also has a mandate to help stateless people.

23

On the Thai border, we saw buses and trucks waiting to take us into camps in Thailand. At that moment, the UN personnel crossed the border and made gestures to come over.

We hesitated at first. When the soldiers did not say anything, we asked them if we could go. They did not say anything, so we went across.

My mother trusted these "white" people who called us to cross the border into Thailand, and so we ran toward their buses and trucks. I had no idea where we were going.

All of my brothers and my mother got on the truck. The vehicle was crammed and there were no seats for us. It was standing room only and we held onto whatever we could. I was not even sure how long the trip was, but when it stopped, we were at a camp.

This place was called *Khao I Dang* (K.I.D). I looked around and saw thousands of people in the K.I.D. camp. The truck dropped us off, and we stood in line to get medicine. Each one of us got two pills and one shot. We did not know what kind of medicine it was and we did not care. We just wanted to get across the border.

They asked all of us to move in further from the drop off zone. It was exciting, but also scary at the same time. Now that we were here, we did not know where we would end up. Was this the beginning or was this the end of my journey?

There were a lot of questions and uncertain feelings, but I kept on persuading myself that whatever it came to, I would have to live with it. There may have been directions and explanations of where we were going, but it was not passed down to us.

We could not understand what people were saying to us and we tried to figure out the gestures that people made to us. When we saw other people had crossed the border to Thailand, we went with them as well. Some of the gestures have different meanings in different cultures.

For example, in Cambodian culture, when we called someone, our palm gesture is facing down, rather than up like in the Western culture. At first, we had no idea if the staff was calling us to cross into Thailand or what their signals meant.

Once we were inside the area, the UNHCR distributed blue plastic sheets to all of the refugees. I did not know why they were in blue, but we thanked the UN for giving us something to cover our heads. They also gave us rice, sardines and dried fish. Water was also distributed to all of us right away.

It was the first time that we had enough water to drink and the first time in many months that we had enough rice to eat. The food was delicious. There was nothing to compare this experience to, and I felt like I was on top of the world.

This camp was one big open space. There was nothing there except for dead grass, bushes and a lot of small trees. My mother and I managed to break down some small trees and tied up the blue tarp.

All of us went in our little shelter because it was too hot outside. Even though we stayed under the tarp, it was still sweltering because we were in an open field.

Whenever I think back to this time, I remember being excited that I was free and living in the refugee camp. It was like waking up from the dead.

IN THE NEXT COUPLE OF DAYS, the UNHCR divided us into sections. My family was in section two. Small houses had been set up in the camp. The houses were built from bamboo and the roofs were made of coconut leaves.

All of the houses in the refugee camp were in rows facing each other. The back end of my house faced someone else's backyard. Between the backyards there was a small canal which led to a larger canal to carry water out in case of rain. People poured water from washing and everything else down this small canal.

Inside each house, there was a bamboo bed the length of the house on one side. It was raised above ground. It was the first time in many months that we able to sleep above ground and in a dry place.

It felt good.

Every day the UN trucks came to the refugee camp and brought water and food to us. It was a big relief, but at the same time it was also sad and a little scary. We still did not know what was going to happen to all of us if the UN stopped coming.

We did not trust the Thai soldiers at all. We did not know exactly who was in charge of the refugee camp. In the morning we saw UN personnel come to work, but at night we saw them go back out. The Thai soldiers came in at night and they were pretty much in control of the refugee camp. The refugees in the camp were at their mercy.

Every day each family received rice, sardines and dried baby bluefish. Every day, the food was the same. If we wanted something different, we could buy it on the black market run by the Thai and a few Cambodians, but we did not have any money to buy anything.

ONE DAY, TWO OF BROTHERS, Marin and Marith, and I saw an elder in the camp carving birds from wood and we watched him doing it. When we got back home, we tried it ourselves, but it did not come out right. We kept on trying for many months.

K.I.D camp was situated near a mountain, but that area was not accessible to us refugees. The camp was surrounded by barbed wire and there were Thai soldiers patrolling the perimeter. From time to time, we snuck out of the camp and up to the mountain to cut down wood to make the carved birds. We kept on practicing creating the birds until we got them perfect. We were not sure what kind of wood it was, but we got it from the mountain near the refugee camp.

Once we had made a few birds, we sold them to the UN personnel and to the Thai workers in the camp. Once the bird was carved, string was attached to the stick and the birds were polished, but not stained because we did not have anything to stain the carved birds. My brother Ka carried it to the front gate of the camp where UN personnel and other workers worked. People bought them as gifts or souvenirs.

It was the first time that we managed to make a little bit of money. The money from selling the birds was used to buy meat, clothes and slippers in the black market.

To be honest, I believe my brother Ka had the hardest job. He stood at the gate for many hours. Sometimes, he was there from morning until evening selling the birds. He would not come back to the house until he had sold the birds, because he knew that we would just ask him to go back and stand there.

Looking back, I felt sorry for him, but we had to do it. He never had any clothes to change. He never had any new shirts. He didn't even have shoes or slippers. All he had on was a pair of shorts. He never complained, which made me feel worse, even though, for many months, he walked back and forth at the gate selling the birds so we could have money.

We were able to buy a few changes of clothes, and occasionally we were able to buy meat and vegetables to eat. It was a struggle just to meet our needs each day. Even though we did not have meat or vegetables, we had enough rice to eat. Thank God for that.

Besides money to buy food and clothes, I wanted some money to buy English textbooks and to pay for English lessons. We wanted to study English so much, but in the end we could not afford it.

WITHIN SIX TO SEVEN MONTHS of our arrival in the camp, the Thais put up barbed wire fences around the camp and towers to watch us in the camp. During the day, there were United Nations workers in the camp, but at night, they left for other towns. At night, the soldiers came in the camp roaming around and doing whatever they felt like doing. This included beatings and even killing people.

In this camp, the refugees had no rights. Or at least if we had rights, they certainly did not pass down to us. We were at the mercy of whomever controlled or patrolled the camp every night.

When I was there, one of the soldiers shot and killed a refugee man. None of us knew why. The body was taken away, and nothing was ever done about it.

If they captured any people outside of the camp, they would punish them severely. After tying them down, they would beat and kick them. It was scary. It intimidated me, but somehow my other brothers and I kept sneaking out into the mountains to get wood to make birds, knowing that if we got caught we would get beaten or possibly killed.

One day our fear came true. I was caught by the Thai Rangers and I thought I was going to die. There were about ten Rangers, and one of them pointed his M-16 rifle at my head. I had no idea what he said because we did not speak the same language. There was a lot of shouting, gun pointing and kicking. I was with about ten people, but in the end, all these Rangers wanted were money and I did not have any.

They held me for a little while; then they released me. I was a little kid and maybe I looked harmless to them. As soon as they made the gesture for me to go, I ran toward the camp. From then on, I never went outside the camp again.

24

There was nothing to do in the refugee camp. I could not go anywhere except to a friend's house or to hang around the hospital that the UN built. The only hope now was that some of the UN and Thai workers would give me some money because I looked so pathetic to them.

There was a school which was supported by the UN at the camp that taught the Khmer language. I attended the school and started to learn to read and write my own language. It was fun.

The UN also passed out toothpaste and toothbrushes. It was the first time in about five years that now I owned a toothbrush. I kept on brushing my teeth.

In this school, there were a lot of students. Most of them came to school not to learn, but because they wanted the hygiene products, pencils, T-shirts, pens and books that the UN provided. Although I enjoyed learning at first, my interest was not in the Khmer language. I wanted to learn English, but English lessons cost money and that I did not have.

I went all over the camp looking for English classes. Some of the English classes were being taught in an open space, but some were in rooms with walls. These were closed to outsiders. If I found any English classes taught outside, I stood around to watch them, hoping that I would learn a few words. I did learn a few words here and there, but most of the time I did not know what those words meant.

Hanging around at the hospital also paid off one day. I got to know one Canadian man whose name was John. I do not recall his last name. I did not speak any English, but making signs helped us to understand each other. I was able to explain to him that I wanted him to buy me an English textbook. Eventually, he did just that. He bought me an English book called, *Oxford English Book I*. I was very happy.

With my book in hand, I went to one of the English teachers and attended a one hour lesson. I paid the instructor one *Bath*, a unit of Thai currency. In 1980, the exchange rate was one dollar was equal to twenty bath, so my lesson was worth about five cents.

I did not learn anything, but at least I had the chance to attend one session. I remember that I tried to use English words with the UN workers. They never could understand what I was saying.

While we were staying in the refugee camp, we saw a lot of people leaving the camp and going to the "third countries," a term which referred to countries outside of Thailand. In 1980, my mother found a sponsor in the United States. This Cambodian woman contacted the International Institute of Rhode Island and they became our official sponsors.

Life for us could have been very different. Instead of southern New England, we could have lived "Down Under." My mother also filed an affidavit with the Australian Embassy. We did not hear anything from them.

After waiting for about a year, my mother's name was posted on the bulletin board in the refugee camp to come to the United States of America. We were jumping with joy. My mother had tears in her eyes. Every day, she went to check the bulletin board and on this particular day, her dream came true. We would be leaving the refugee camp and going to the United States.

IN MARCH OF 1981, the Immigration and Naturalization Service (INS) called my mother in to be interviewed. Once the process began, it took only a few weeks to leave the Khao I Dang camp where we had lived for two years. The bus took us to Mairot, another refugee camp, to be interviewed.

All the people in this camp had their names posted to leave for the "third countries." We stayed in this camp for three months and were interviewed almost every week. The INS asked so many questions.

What was our dates of birth? Were any American soldiers in Cambodia? Did we have any living relatives left? Were we Khmer Rouge or not?

We also had to sign a lot of papers and fill out many forms. We had no idea what most of them were all about. When our family arrived at the refugee camp in Thailand, my mother's and our birthdays became very important in the process of coming to the United States. The

Immigration and Naturalization Service (INS) required accurate birth dates.

For this reason, she made birthdays up very quickly for all of us. She gave my birthday as June 4, 1966, my four brothers birthdays were given as: Marin, August 6, 1968; Marith, March 3, 1970; Ka, February 2, 1972; and Ra. May 5, 1975. These dates were chosen because they were easy to remember.

My mother was required to give all of these dates to the INS during the interview that she had. I cannot recall either my brothers or me telling the INS of our birth dates.

Every week the same questions were asked, but there would be a different person looking for answers. They spoke English, but were accompanied by a translator. They provided no indication of when we would be able to leave the camp.

AT MAIROT, there were also barbed wire fences surrounding the camp. The houses were built in rows. There were four rows that were connected to each other to form a square. All of the houses faced each other with one common playground. It was all sand, and there were no trees. In the middle of the playground, there was a well – but the water was very dirty.

In general, conditions were better. The house was a little bit nicer. This time it was built of wood, not bamboo. We received more food and plenty of water. There were many water storage tanks nearby.

We did not have to stand in lines for water as we did in Khao I Dang. We could go any time to get water to drink or to bathe. Once in a while, the Thai guards opened the gate and allowed all of us to go to the beach.

There were also more activities in this camp. The soldiers always asked the Cambodian men to play soccer with them. When they played, all the other people would come to watch.

Every morning, the soldiers put on the Thai National Anthem and we had to get up to salute the Thai flag. In the evening, they repeated the music. Despite the pledge, most people, including my family, looked forward to going to the beach and to seeing the soccer game, but most of all to leaving for America. When we passed all the interviews, we left that camp and went on to the next camp. It was called "Transit."

We were on our way – or so we thought.

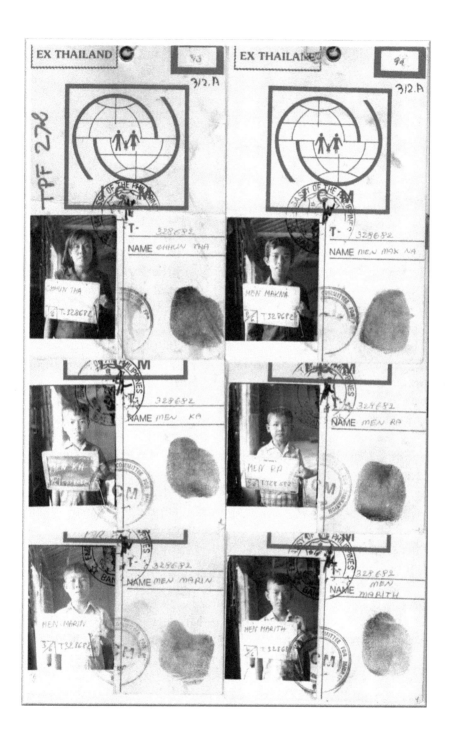

25

When we arrived at this camp, we were supposed to stay only for a few days, but my brothers and I were not on the list to come to the United States. Somehow, they had only forwarded my mother's name.

We wondered if we would be separated after all this time of fighting to stay together. We were so worried.

We had to stay in this camp for two weeks before they straightened it out. My mother went to see the INS personnel and begged them to speed up the process. We just wanted to get out.

Finally, our names reappeared and they took us to another camp. This camp was called *Lomphiny*. Again, we were supposed to be there for only a few days. We were told the next step was to board the airplane to the United States.

Just as our hopes grew, something happened again.

As we prepared to leave, my brother Ka developed a growth on his face just below his eyes. It looked like a big pimple, but it was about the size of a plum. They stopped our journey, even though all of us passed the physical examination except Ka.

All of us had to stay behind in Bangkok.

We were stuck there for about three weeks. At one time this camp was a prison. It had not gotten much better.

The place was very smelly and it was very dirty. All of the Cambodian refugees who lived in this camp were sealed off from the Thai people. We might as well have been in jail.

During the third week, my brother Ka had to go to see the doctor. As soon as he got there, three people held him down and they cut the giant pimple open.

It was all infected.

These people did not use any anesthetic on him and he screamed so loud with pain. Who knew if these men were really medical technicians or not? It might not have been the best medical care, but the procedure worked. A few days later, my family was cleared and allowed to board the airplane.

I thought we were bound for the United States, but we landed in the Philippines.

NO ONE TOLD US that we were going to the Philippines, but after about a three hour flight from Bangkok, Thailand, there we were in the Philippines.

When the airplane landed, there were many buses waiting to take us to another camp. It was toward the evening. We boarded the bus and food was given to us in a package. I ate some of it because I was hungry – but I also did not feel good from the journey.

The bus took us over narrow roads that passed by mountains and cliffs to a camp. We had no idea where we were going. All I knew was that it took a long time to get to the camp.

And the road was rough.

The road we travelled was very narrow and it seemed like we were driving through the mountains. But there was many cliffs. I was so scared. With each pitch and turn, I was afraid that the bus would go off the road into the valley below.

Everyone was sick with motion sickness and everyone began vomiting. I tried to help my brothers and my mother, because somehow, I was not sick.

We finally arrived at the camp around midnight. The workers in the camp came out to greet us and took us to our quarters. Soon we found out that the reason why we ended up in the Philippines was because we did not know any English.

We stayed in the Philippines for about five months in 1981. We were supposed to learn English and the American way of life there. My mother and all of us had to go to school and were put on the work program.

I worked in the school and my job was to help translate English into Khmer for children. I was actually more like a teacher's aide. Even though I did not speak much English, I still wanted to work in a classroom.

It was a task, and there was no significance to it. Little did I know at the time that my career would be in education.

Every time we went to work, we got stamps in our book. When we finished our program, we would be able to get out and come to the United States. I enjoyed staying in the Philippines, except for a minor earthquake.

We had enough food to eat and plenty of water to drink. We received chicken, pork and vegetables each day.

The best part about this camp was that we could go anywhere. There were no barbed wire fences surrounding the camp and there were no restrictions on us. Every day after work, another Cambodian and I went to bathe in the waterfall. It was a lot of fun.

While we were living in the Philippines, we still carved birds from wood to sell. It was much easier to get wood in the mountains. We sold the birds we made to the Filipinos and to other workers in the camp. With the money we received, we bought flip flops, pants and shirts.

Before we left for the United States, my family was able to save seven dollars. My mother wanted to have some money with us in case we needed to buy food along the way. We had no idea what the trip was going to be like, but we wanted to be prepared.

When we were living in the Philippines, we had to go through physical examinations. We had to take a lot of medicines. I did not know what they were, but all of us had to take the pills and receive vaccines or else we could not be allowed to go the United States. At least that's what the rumor was.

When it was time, we wanted to be prepared for the United States, both mentally and physically.

26

On December 14, 1981, we left the Philippines for the United States. I was seventeen years old. There were so many things going through my head. I was frightened, but I was also happy.

The bus came into the camp and took us to Manila, the capital city of the Philippines. When we arrived at the airport, we had to wait for a few hours before boarding the World Airways plane. Most of the people in the airplane were refugees, and there were hundreds waiting to board.

We could see the aircraft and it was scary. The plane was so big that it had two floors. I had never seen anything this big before. I was afraid to get on. How could an airplane this huge and carrying so many people on board fly?

It did.

The plane took off safely and our first stop was Hong Kong. While we were in the plane, the stewardess gave us a meal. It was good. When we landed in Hong Kong, they told all of us to wait in the airplane.

I looked out the airplane windows and saw the city. It was so beautiful. We were in another world. The world that we never knew.

An hour later we left Hong Kong. We were on the airplane for many more hours and we had many meals. Most of the time we were in the dark. After many hours, we finally landed in Alaska and it was still dark.

From Alaska we flew several more hours before we landed again in San Francisco. By the time we landed, it was day time. The trip from the Philippines to San Francisco probably took about twenty-one hours.

The buses came out onto the tarmac and they asked all of the people to get aboard. They checked the tags that we brought with us from the Philippines. The buses took us to Oakland.

We were finally in the United States.

CALIFORNIA WAS A LONG WAY from Cambodia – both in terms of distance and opportunity. I was not sure why we stayed there, but they told us to stay there.

And so we waited. But honestly, I was in another world.

Again, food was good. They had rice, vegetables and chicken. Food and water were plentiful. We had plenty to eat and plenty of water in which to bathe.

Our lives were very different only a few months ago. Our world had opened up, but our future was uncertain, because we had not reached our destination yet.

At night, I sat outside the housing complex watching the city lights, mesmerized by this world. So many times I could not believe that I was there, watching and wondering.

How could this be? Was I really dreaming? Was I free of suffering?

It was beautiful. I got to play basketball and football. At first, I did not know what football was. I tried to kick it, but it did not go. I said to myself, "Why did they make a football that could not even be kicked?"

I put the football down and decided to play basketball instead. During my stay in Oakland, an agency passed out coats for people who were going to cold climates. All of us received a coat, but not sneakers. They only had one kind of coat, so all of us looked the same. The coat was black with a green stripe.

When we left Oakland, we went back to the San Francisco airport and we stayed there for many hours. Someone from the airport asked my family to stay put in one corner. Being new to the country, we were afraid of everything.

So we did what we were told.

No one came to give us food or drink. After so many years in the camps, we expected people to feed us. We had no idea that we were expected to fend for ourselves.

We sat there for many hours. We did not go anywhere because we could not speak English and we did not want to do anything wrong. We were afraid, but we were also thirsty and hungry.

I saw a water fountain and I wanted to go to get a drink so badly, but I was afraid. I saw people walk by and I watched the water come out. I sat there watching it.

Over and over, I kept saying to myself and to my brothers that I was going to take a chance to get water for us, but with what? I walked there and I walked back.

Nobody said anything to me. I would do it again and again.

Finally, I decided to take a drink. I got a little bit of water and I ran back. Next, my brothers, one by one, ran over to the water fountain and took drinks. We did not know the water was there for everyone to drink.

NOW, THINKING BACK, that fear was the reality of a newcomer. There is no shame to it. Sometimes we think that people should know about the water fountain, but if the person comes from another culture where water was not plentiful, people would think that it was not free. One culture may look at it differently.

Helping people to understand that would be part of my life's work.

We boarded Eastern Airlines and left for Providence, Rhode Island. The only refugee family on the airplane was my family. The airplane landed in Atlanta, Georgia and we had to change planes.

When we came out of the airplane, there was one lady who waited for us. She was Chinese-American. She spoke Chinese to my mother. My mother did not speak any Chinese. She left us alone, but she took us to another gate in the airport.

We boarded another Eastern Airlines jet, and after many hours, we arrived at Green Airport on December 16, 1981. It was close to midnight. We were back in the dark – again.

Map in the public domain.

Providence, Rhode Island

Providence is the capital and most populous city in Rhode Island. Founded in 1636, it is one of the oldest cities in the United States. It is located in Providence County, and is the third-largest city in the New England region after Boston and Worcester. Providence was founded by Roger Williams, a religious exile from the Massachusetts Bay Colony. He named the area in honor of "God's merciful Providence" which he believed was responsible for revealing such a haven for him and his followers to settle.

27

There were a lot of people waiting for us at Green Airport. It was a happy moment. For the first time since we made our journey out of the Philippines, we met someone that we could talk to. Most importantly, we met our sponsors.

The five of us were in our flip flops, a pair of pants, a shirt and a coat. Yes, we looked horrible. Our sponsors took us to their car and we left for their house.

Outside of the airport, there was this white stuff on the ground. We asked them what it was and they told us that it is snow. It was cold. Despite all the snow, it was beautiful.

About twenty minutes later, we arrived at our sponsors' house on Chapin Avenue in Providence. Our sponsors had cooked a lot of food for us, but we could not eat. Maybe it was the excitement, or maybe it was the long hectic trip that we had.

For me, I know it was the excitement. I knew in my heart that I was finally free. I wanted to go to school. That was on my mind.

There were a lot of people who came to the house to greet us. In the morning, our sponsors took us to Assumption Church to look for sneakers, shirts, sweaters and coats. That was where my family met Sister Angela Daniels and Father Daniel Trainor. Since the Assumption Church did not have any sneakers and coats at the time, Sister Angela Daniels took my brothers and me to a store.

We didn't know what the building was or even what a "store" was. All I know is that the place was nice. It was the first time that I entered any store. We got socks, sneakers and coats. I will never forget their generosity toward my family.

A few months later, I carved the wood birds and I drew them a picture of Angkor Wat as an expression of my sincere appreciation.

OUR NEW LIVES STARTED THE NEXT DAY. My mother went to the Rhode Island Welfare Department to apply for Assistance to

Families with Dependent Children (AFDC) and Food Stamps. In the meantime, we continued to stay at the sponsors' house.

As soon as we received the first check, we rented a third floor apartment across Chapin Avenue from the sponsors' house. The Assumption Church donated used beds, chairs, tables and furniture to us. For the first time in seven years, we had our own home and were able to cook our own food.

We had only a few pieces of furniture in the house and the dining table was used for many years – even after we moved from that house to Waverly Street in Providence. The house that we lived in had only central heating unit and it was in the living room. At night, it was very cold in the bedrooms. All of my brothers and my mother slept in the living room around the heat. The floor was a hardwood floor and it was cold because we did not have enough blankets.

Despite the challenges, I was happy that my family lived in one place and we had enough food to eat. A couple of weeks later, Brother Joseph Desrochers, also from Assumption Church, took my brothers and me to take the required tests to enter school. Once again, we had to go through physical examinations and be given shots.

The tests given to us was to test our knowledge. The school department wanted to know how much English we knew and our general knowledge of the world. At the time, we did not understand what was going on.

Based on the test, Marin was assigned to the Samuel W. Bridgham Middle School and my other three brothers went to George J. West Elementary School in Providence, Rhode Island. I was assigned to Central High School. If I was actually born in 1964, that made me an eighteen year old. I believe that the assignment of school was based on age – I don't think it was because of what I knew or how well I did on the test.

Although I was looking forward to my first day of school, at the same time I was very sad and very nervous about the experience. I did not know how many Cambodian students were in the school. There were a lot of questions going on in my head. It was the first time that I would receive any formal education since I attended school in Cambodia, and that was only up to fourth grade. To make things even worse, I did not speak much English. But here I was, starting my education during the third quarter of freshman year at Central High School. I did not know what to expect.

CENTRAL HIGH SCHOOL IN PROVIDENCE is an old public building on a busy street in the city. I had never seen anything like it before when I walked through the main entrance at around 7:45 a.m. on January 18, 1982.

The first thing I saw at the door was a group of students standing there. Why they were laughing? I wondered, could it be the way I was dressed? I soon found out.

As I walked past them, one of the students spat on my head and everyone in the group started laughing even louder. I learned my first lesson: hatred.

Who knew that the shirt I had on was a woman's blouse? It was another cultural fact that women's blouses have button on the left and that men's shirts have buttons on the right. I learned that lesson the hard way.

I had tears in my eyes, and I did not know where to go or to whom I should report the incident. Instead, I just walked into the school. I cleaned myself up with my hands.

Once inside the building, I saw some other Cambodian students and told them what happened. They took me to the bathroom to get cleaned up.

When the bell rang, I had to go class, but I was lost in the school. I did not know what to do. There were a few Cambodian students in the school and they showed me where my classes were. Since I spoke very little English, I spent three periods a day in English as a Second Language (ESL) classes and, during the other three periods, I had gym, math and drawing. I passed every class in that half year.

In September of 1982, when school started again, I had more ESL classes, but the number was reduced to two periods a day. In the meantime I also applied to the Upward Bound Program at Rhode Island College with my two friends, Chanthol and Sarith. When we were accepted into the program, my friends and I were very happy.

Upward Bound is a program that helps high school students from low income families prepare for colleges and universities. During the initial stage of the program, we had to stay after school for extra help with homework. Also, on Saturday, we had to go to the college from eight o'clock in the morning until noon.

Sometimes we walked to school. Other times, we stayed at a friend's house and he dropped us off. If we walked, it took us about one hour to get home from the college, which was six to eight miles away. It was very cold and the streets were very slippery.

At that time we dressed poorly because we could not afford to buy any new clothes or sneakers. Whatever clothes we had we got from Assumption Church or the Salvation Army. We could not afford to buy new things because we were on welfare, and we did not have enough money.

At about the same time, I was involved with the Assumption Church a great deal. Almost every Sunday I went to church and after the church service I usually went with the church personnel to help move furniture at people's houses or move things from church to church.

We didn't have much, but we were happy to help the people who helped us assist others.

WHEN SUMMER FINALLY ARRIVED, I was so happy. I was glad not only because it was warm, but because I was scheduled to live at the college for a six week Upward Bound program. I expected that it would be hard, but I hoped that it would be fun, too.

It was both, but I worked very hard that summer and it paid off because I won the Director's Award for overall performance. That summer the program gave out only one award and I received it. It was the proudest moment in my life.

It came as a surprise because I did not expect anything. I knew that I worked very hard in all my subjects because I wanted to learn, but I was not prepared for an award. I did not ask my mother to go and, even worse, I did not have any new clothes to wear for the occasion. There were a lot of people there.

In my third year, I left ESL classes and went into regular classes. I wanted to take Business English at high school, but I had to go to talk to my Guidance Counselor first and then to my ESL teacher to get out of ESL classes. At first, my teacher said that I could not do the work required in a regular class. It would be too difficult for me. I insisted that I should be able try it out.

After a couple of days of going back and forth between the counselor and the teacher, I finally got in, but on a trial basis. I worked very hard in that English class, because I wanted to prove that I could do the work. At the end of the year, I finished with a "B" average. I did book reports and research papers.

It was difficult, but I spent four to five hours each night learning English and doing homework. I translated almost every single English word into Khmer. On top of each English word, I wrote in Khmer the pronunciation and on top of the pronunciation, I wrote the meaning. I never got to go out during that school year. All I did was spend a lot of time studying, and figuring out the meaning and the pronunciation of words.

In my last year at Central High School, I took Business English again, but at a different level. In the whole class, I was the only Asian student. When the teacher asked me to read, I was very nervous.

When I read, the other students in class usually laughed at me because of my pronunciation. When I started reading, I would begin to sweat and my face turned pale. I felt chills and hot flashes on my face and body. I was afraid of the whole situation and it was quite an experience.

In the two years that I spent in regular classes, I never spoke a word to any students in my courses. It was not that I did not like them, but I could not bring myself to talk to them because many of them laughed at me all the time. I wanted to make friends with other students, but I did not want to be embarrassed if they said "no" to me. I was very lonely.

Throughout my high school years, I had only a few American friends because they went to Upward Bound with me. In 1985, I graduated from Central High School, and was ranked fifth in my class of about 280 students. I was also named to the Rhode Island Honor Society and received the Presidential Academic Fitness Award.

Not bad for a Cambodian kid who didn't know much three and a half years before.

28

Toward the end of the summer of 1985, my mother got very sick one night. She vomited non-stop. The next morning, I took her to St. Joseph's Hospital on Broad Street, but the doctor sent her home. When she got home, she lay flat on the floor. She was exhausted and she could not eat.

I knew that she was very sick, but I could not understand why the doctor sent her home. The second night, around midnight, she started to vomit again. It was very serious. She could hardly move.

I got scared.

I wanted to call the ambulance or the rescue, but I was afraid to call them. I was very reluctant, but what convinced me to call was when I saw that my mother did not move. She looked exhausted on the floor of the living room. I decided to call the rescue.

About five minutes later, the rescue van arrived with the siren on. I went downstairs to open the door for them. I was very happy that they came so quickly. They stopped in front of my house, but no one came out. A few minutes later, two men walked out and the older man yelled at me, "Why didn't you call a taxi? Why did you call us?"

I was in shock. I could not respond to him. He said it so loud that it looked like I was arguing with him. One of my brothers heard the noise and he ran downstairs and my dog also came down. My dog started to bark at them.

The man who yelled at me now held a walkie-talkie and he threatened to kill my dog if he did not stop barking. My brother took the dog back upstairs, put him in the bedroom, and locked the door.

I stood angrily on the porch in front of the house waiting for the rescuer to go up to see my mother. I kept telling them that my mother was very sick.

Maybe they did not understand what I was saying but they were ignoring me completely. They finally came upstairs and they told me and my brothers to take her down the stairs. We did and I went into the rescue van with her. They did not turn on the siren and they took off casually toward St. Joseph Hospital.

The older man sat in the back of the rescue with my mother and me. My mother was not lying down. Nobody said anything to us, so I tried to hang on to her as we were sitting on the rescue's bed. The rescue worker sat toward the front of the rescue and he kept staring at me and my mother. He looked so mean, which made me very nervous and scared. I did not know what he was going to say or do to us.

A few minutes later he asked if we had an insurance card and I handed him my mother's medical card and he made a comment about it, "On Welfare!"

WHEN WE ARRIVED AT THE HOSPITAL, I escorted my mother to the emergency room. They went in after us. The older man told the nurse that we were on Welfare. They started to talk to each other. The nurse did not ask any questions or come to look at my mother.

I felt like we were invisible in their eyes as I stood there supporting my mother while they chatted. It took them a long time to take a look at my mother. I was furious, but I controlled myself. I did not say a word to them. I waited patiently until they were ready to take care of my mother.

The nurse came and took our statements and the insurance card and then she sent my mother inside to be examined by the doctor. As soon as my mother got inside, the doctor examined her. After a few hours, the doctor sent her home. When she got home, she still did not feel any better.

We decided to call our sponsors and asked for their help. They came and took my mother back to the hospital. This time we went in their car. When we got there, the doctor put my mother on intravenous fluids immediately and admitted her.

When I came home around four in the morning, I was still furious at the situation. I called the fire department, not knowing who I was speaking to, to complain about the incident that took place at my house, but the person who picked up the phone told me to call back in the morning. I did not call back the next morning, because I went to see my mother in the hospital.

Although I wanted to call back, I thought that it would be my word against theirs, and that nobody was going to believe me. Now, I regret that I did not call back. I should have called back because that man should never have worked as a rescuer because of his prejudice against other races.

In a short period of time in the United States, I learned many lessons that I never thought existed in this world.

When I think back, what stopped me from calling back that day was that I did not speak English very well and I did not know the law. That man took advantage of my family dearly because we were Cambodians.

Despite all of the things that took place, my mother became well again and three days later she left the hospital. I never did find out what was wrong with her. From that moment on, even today, my mother is scared of going to the hospital – and she certainly does not want me to call any Emergency Medical Technicians.

I never got over this anger. I could not believe that there were people out there who could do such a thing to an ill person.

29

After graduating from Central High School, I went to Rhode Island College and was accepted by the Preparatory Enrollment Program (PEP) at the college. My English skills were still not that great, so they put me in ESL classes at the college. I enrolled on Saturday and took evening classes to learn English. For the first year, I received only a few college credits. It was not until my second year that I received full college credits.

College was very difficult, especially for me because I did not speak English well enough and my writing was very poor. I wanted to quit school many times that year. I was not sure if I could do college work because the courses were too difficult.

In addition to the challenges of learning English, I was very lonely because I did not have many friends. I lived in the dormitory, but I did not really get along with the other students because they were wild. My behavior was completely different from other students in the suite. I was quiet and polite. I liked to go to sleep early, but sometimes it was almost impossible. When I was living in the dormitory, I met another Cambodian student, Vilai Or, and we became best friends.

Every day I had to study. I never seemed to have time to do things in my life. I had to study two to three times harder than other students. I was confused day to day with what I was supposed to do. I felt very sad.

On top of this, I did not know where I could turn for help. I could not talk to my mother about how I felt, and I did not know where to go in the college, except to my classes and back to the dormitory. At the time, counseling was a new concept for me, and I did not know how to get the help I needed.

Because of the circumstances that I faced at the college, I started to associate with people who were like me, and I got involved with the Cambodian community. In addition to support and friendship, I saw a need in the community. I tried to help other Cambodians, especially students in high school in Providence.

When I was in college, I had a lot of concerns for my family at home and for myself. For one thing, I did not speak English very much and I did not know if I could do college work. Another reason was that I was worried that I did not have any money. I was no longer on welfare and I wanted to go to work to help my family, but at the same time, I wanted to go to school.

FOR A LONG TIME, I WAS TORN between helping my family and helping myself. Despite the hardship, I passed all of my classes for the first year. At the end of my first year, I received twelve credits. The reason that I received twelve credits instead of twenty four, was because I still took a lot of English as a Second Language classes.

One day, I asked a few of my friends to help organize a group of students to go to high schools to explain what should be taken when they were still in school and what they could expect when they arrived at the college. I chose students in Providence to work with because I had gone through the system and I knew how hard it was to get help, both academically and emotionally. We reached a lot of students in three of the high schools in Providence and it was very successful. We did this voluntarily.

For two years we had graduation parties for high school graduates and the Cambodian Society of RI, Inc. picked up the cost. At the graduation party, either my friend or I got up to speak and to encourage the graduates to continue their education beyond high school.

We had a lot of Cambodian food to share with parents and friends. Also, we provided entertainment and awards to the graduates.

One year we had a graduation party at Rhode Island College, and there were 57 high school students who graduated from schools throughout Rhode Island. Almost half of those graduates went on to either two year or four year colleges or universities. I was very happy.

Also, when I was at the college, I started an Asian Student Association Club with the help of Jeff Kenyon, a counselor for Upward Bound. I was elected as president of the club throughout my college years. It was because of my involvement in all of these activities and Jeff Kenyon's encouragement – who remains my friend to this day that I stayed in college.

Besides the activities with Cambodian youth, I also got involved with the Cambodian Society of RI, Inc. In fact, I was appointed to sit on their Board of Education for two years. I taught the Khmer language in their summer program to many Cambodian youngsters. I thought that this would be one of the important aspects of keeping culture my alive. Many of the children who were born in the United States or born in the refugee camps had no idea how to write their own language or to comprehend their own culture.

This picture were taken in 1990 in an apartment on Waverly Street in Providence, RI. Left to right – Marith, Marin, Tha Chhun (mom), Samoutta (wife), Makna, Ka and in the front, Ra.

30

In December of 1981, the most beautiful person came into my life, Samoutta Iem. We met the second day I arrived in Rhode Island. I was about 18 and I was sitting in my immigration sponsor's living room on Chapin Avenue in Providence, RI.

She was the first person I saw. She was wearing a blue skirt and a white blouse. As she moved around the room, my eyes followed her everywhere. My chest was pounding, my stomach was flipping and I could not figure out why. I was afraid to get close to her.

Come to find out, it was love; love at first sight.

Both of us attended Central High School in Providence, RI. I was one year ahead of her class. Every day I stalked her, knowing exactly when she would be at her locker. I was careful to not let her know that I was following her. Every opportunity that I could, I followed her from Central High School to her home, just to be sure that she was safe. Even though we hardly spoke to one another, I was thrilled just to see her and to walk close to her.

Even though we knew each other and went to the same school, I did not really talk to her. I only began talking to her when I went to Central High School to talk to students about colleges and then I approached her. At the time, she was a senior. From then on, I called her and we talked on the phone.

It was the beginning of a long and loving relationship.

IN APRIL OF 1986, I asked my mother to talk to Samoutta's mother. We wanted to get married because we loved each other and wanted to have a family. At the time, she was a teacher's assistant with the Attleboro Public Schools and I was a full-time student at Rhode Island College.

122

One Saturday that month, my mother went to her house to meet her mother and they talked. When my mother returned, she told me that her mother had no objection to our engagement, but she had to ask her daughter first. About a week later, her mother told my mother that she agreed. On June 26, 1986, we got engaged.

We started our engagement very early in the morning. Two nights before the engagement my mother bought a lot of fruits and cakes. She put them in a tray and wrapped them up beautifully in thin, clear, colorful plastic.

My friends arrived at my house early in the morning, and they packed up the cars with those fruits. Her house was only about three blocks away. When we arrived at her house, there were about 30 people waiting for us. We took the fruit up to the second floor and we arranged the fruit in pairs in the living room.

I sat in the living with the guests and they asked me a lot of questions:

Are you in school? What are you studying? What are your plans for the future?

This lasted for about half an hour before Samoutta came out and the engagement process began. She gave me an eighteen karat gold bracelet that weighed about an ounce and I gave her the diamond ring. The exchange of dowries became a symbol that we were engaged. All of the guests who were present at our engagement ceremony were our witnesses.

I liked Samoutta the first time I saw her, and I did not want people to talk about us. That was why I asked for an engagement. Once the engagement was done, people would not talk about us as much when they saw us in public.

After our engagement, I went back to school, and Samoutta continued her study at Central High School. We did not see each other as much because I was in college. In the evening, I could call her at home. We kept our relationship going this way until we got married.

IN THE SUMMER OF 1988, my friend Arn Chorn-Pond and I got jobs as intern reporters for the *Providence Journal.* That summer, we wrote at least eight articles. A few of them made the front page. It was a good feeling. We got to know the people inside the *Journal* and met many others that summer.

One day when we were at work, I got a call from Barry Marshall, a drama teacher from Moses Brown School in Providence. He wanted to talk to my friend and me about our lives, especially, during the Communist regime in Cambodia.

At first, I was a bit hesitant, but my friend talked me into it. After work that evening, we met Barry in front of the *Journal* building, and then, we went to the park to talk. Barry explained to us what he was looking for and we agreed to talk to him.

The next day, after work, we went to Moses Brown and we started to talk about our past. Many weeks later, he brought in seven more people, including a script writer, W.E.R LaFarge. We worked on telling our story. Some of us were crying, and we were comforting each other.

Scene by scene, Mr. Marshall and Mr. LaFarge put together a play of about 45 minutes subtitled, *I Never Talked About This*. It was a hit in our community. We performed at many high and middle schools in Providence. We also performed in the community and at churches. Our last show was at the Rhode Island School of Design auditorium in Providence.

From that point on, I was able to talk more about my past experiences. At first, I did not realize that being in the play was part of a healing process. This fact did not come to mind until I attended graduate school in counseling.

I WAS SWORN IN BY A JUDGE as a United States citizen in September of 1988. The *Providence Journal* then asked me to write about my past experience and I did. The next day, my story made the front page of the morning and *Evening Bulletin*. Included in it was a five by seven inch picture of me holding a Naturalization Certificate. I was so happy.

Around Christmas in 1988, I had to ask my mother to talk to Samoutta's mother again, because we wanted to get married.

31

My mother did, and I started to plan the wedding. I went around Rhode Island searching for clubs that I could rent for our reception. The only place that was available was a place called the Opportunity Industrial Center (OIC) in Providence.

I booked the place for Saturday, July 8, 1989, for the price of $1,250.00. From then on, I used my weekends to work on renting tables and chairs and other necessities for the wedding.

On Saturday, July 8, 1989, we got married. Friends and relatives from everywhere came to my house. Some of my relatives came from as far as North Carolina a few days in advance.

Our wedding day started very early. Accompanied by my relatives and my friends, we drove our cars to Samoutta's house to ask for permission to be married. We arrived at her house at about seven o'clock in the morning.

We did not start immediately, because the musicians had not arrived yet. While we were waiting, we were busy as well. Some of my friends were taking fruit baskets out of the cars and vans and placing them on top of the cars ready to carry into her house.

Soon, the five musicians had arrived. They were all dressed in white shirts that were buttoned up all the way to their necks. They looked very professional. Finally we were ready to go.

The musicians started out from a few houses down from her house. Music played at full swing. Many of my friends and relatives lined up in pairs behind the musicians, and we walked toward her house. My friends and I lined up behind the musicians.

That morning we woke up a lot of people in our neighborhood.

WHEN WE GOT TO HER HOUSE, my mother rang the doorbell. Her mother came down and my mother asked if she and all the guests could go in and bring all the fruits and gifts upstairs. We were allowed to go in and the ceremony started.

All of the gifts and fruits were carried in pairs. Each person held a pair of trays or carried a basket in each hand. We had all kinds of gifts. We had clothes, jewelry, apples, bananas, grapes, pears, plums and many different types of canned fruits that were imported from Thailand. Once the gifts were upstairs, we had to lay them out by pairs on the floor in the living room.

My mother and her mother had to talk again about our arrangement in front of all the guests and relatives. Even though the marriage had been agreed to before we got there, the parents on both sides had to discuss the marriage so everybody could hear. It took about half an hour.

Then the wedding ceremony moved to my house because Samoutta's house was too small. When we arrived at my house, my fiance went upstairs with her friends and relatives. At that moment, my house became her house. In the Cambodian culture, all weddings are traditionally done at the girl's house.

Since we had a problem with space, we used my house to accommodate everyone. All of the fruits and gifts that had been brought to her house were moved down and put back in the cars and vans. Once again the guests helped to carry the gifts behind the musicians and all of us paraded down the street to my house.

It was much easier this time, because my mother did not have to ask her mother again. She already had permission for me to be married to her daughter and everyone heard it. We did not have to wait for anything else. Quickly, the musicians went upstairs and so did everyone else.

The weather was hot, but the music was good. I went upstairs and changed from my suit into the traditional clothes. I did not feel very comfortable wearing them because I had never worn them before. The colors and the clothes were established many years ago. The first outfit that I had to wear was green. My fiance was also dressed in green, but in a different style.

We came out to greet our guests and relatives by putting both hands in the prayer position and by bowing a little bit. We had to pay our respects and give thanks to the people who came to our ceremony. Then we went to our rooms and changed into another outfit. This time, the outfits were gold. When we came out this time, the actual ceremony started. It was all over around twelve o'clock.

Makna and Samoutta in the traditional wedding attire in July 8, 1989.

WE RUSHED OUT and left all the guests to eat lunch at my house. The reason that we rushed out was because we had a one o'clock appointment at the *Church of Jesus Christ,* in Cranston, Rhode Island, to be married, and sixty guests were waiting for us there. We had a Christian minister marry us. The church marriage did not take long at all. It was all over around 1:30 in the afternoon.

Then we went to a reception at Phnom Penh restaurant on Elmwood Avenue. We had about 120 people there. We had a live band and they played Christian music. All of our guests were enjoying themselves.

At night, we had another reception at the O.I.C., the hall that we rented in Providence. It was a wild one. We entertained about 420 people that evening. All of our guests were invited by my mother and my wife's relatives. We had a lot of fun, but we were also exhausted.

The party went on until midnight. My wife and I did not get to eat any food because we were too busy greeting our guests and serving them. We went from table to table until we greeted everyone.

At each table, we had to offer a cigarette to each person and thank them for coming. In return, they gave us gifts. The money was sealed in an envelope that had their names on it. The money from the gifts helped pay the expenses that we incurred. We spent about $14,000 dollars for the wedding, but we received gifts of about $16,000. With the money we had left, we bought a car that we used until 1994.

That night after we came back from the club, we stayed at my mother's house. My relatives and my mother's friends were also at my house. It was still packed. They stayed up to talk about my wedding. I had to stay up with them until three in the morning.

We were exhausted, but very happy and now a married couple looking to start our own life.

Makna and Samoutta with their wedding party, July 8, 1989

ABOUT TWO WEEKS LATER, I MOVED OUT of my mother's house to live with my wife at her house. Her brother had just bought a house and they had a room for us. I did not reject the idea because I did not have any money, and I was still in school. I did not work, but my wife did.

I still had another year of college to go, which consisted mostly of teaching practicum and internship. In the fall of 1989, I did my practicum at Nathaniel Green Middle school in Providence. Three times a week, I taught two classes. I was so excited. When I finished my practicum, I received an "A" for it.

IN THE SPRING, I DID MY INTERNSHIP at Central High School under Bob McAdam, the Social Studies Department Head. He was a nice man. We talked a lot about teaching and family. I have the highest respect for him.

Although it was kind of funny returning to my high school, this time as a teacher, I was very happy that I got to do my internship at my high school because I was in the same environment when I was a student there. The teachers that I had when I was a student were still working, so I felt comfortable there.

One day when my internship was almost over, Mr. McAdam and I walked across the street from Central High School to fill out an application for a teaching position with the Providence School Department. I was hoping that I would get a job because there were no Cambodian teachers in the schools that were certified.

My hope turned to despair when I did not get it.

The School Department wanted me to be a substitute teacher, but with my economic disadvantage, I could not wait to be on call. I had to look for something else that would be more stable. I turned it down.

In May of 1990, I graduated from Rhode Island College. I received my Bachelor's degree in Social Science, Secondary Education. It was the proudest moment in my life.

There was nothing to compare my feelings to. My mother and my wife were also very happy.

My mother always said to my brothers and me that she brought us here so we could educate ourselves.

"Knowledge will go a long way," she said. "I do not have anything else to give you. No money, gold or diamonds. All I have for you is another chance in life. Work for it!"

That was enough for all of us.

Map from maps.com in the public domain.

Fall River, Massachusetts

Fall River is the tenth largest city in the Commonwealth, based on the 2010 census. Its 88,857 residents include many people of Portuguese descent. Once the leading textile manufacturing center in the United States, it is still known as the "Spindle City," as well as the "Scholarship City," because Dr. Irving Fradkin started Dollars for Scholars in the city in 1958. The infamous Borden murders took place in Fall River, and it is also the hometown of Emeril Lagasse and the largest collection of World War II Naval vessels.

32

With no job, but with a college degree in hand and my mother's words in mind, I turned to a nearby city, Fall River, Massachusetts. I filled out an application and dropped it off at the School Administration Building on Rock Street.

The offices were located in a former home in what was known as "The Highlands." It was where the mill owners lived and on the same street as the original B.M.C. Durfee High School. This granite building with its clock tower and observatory had been closed in 1978, and a new, modern high school was built on Elsbree Street.

Originally, a wealthy mill town, it was now kind of run down and most of its population was of Portuguese descent. By the 1990s, there were many Cambodians and other Asians moving into the tenement houses that once housed the mill workers.

Lucky for me, nobody in the school department spoke Khmer or had any background in the Southeast Asian experience.

Not long afterward, I had a job interview with the Director of Transitional Bilingual Education in Fall River. At the end of the interview, I was offered a job in an elementary school - I think it was the Carroll School - as a kindergarten teacher with a promise to move to high school.

Although I had never taught little children, I took the job and started in the fall of 1990. I was at this position for about a month before I was asked to go to Durfee High School.

My responsibilities at the high school were varied. I taught U.S. History and Western History and the World.

I was a young man at the time and some of the students who sat in front of me were actually older than me. I think I was about 24 years old when I started teaching.

My age wasn't the only problem. I was also the only Cambodian/Khmer teacher in the building. For the first few weeks, teachers and staff in the building did not know that I was a teacher.

Every time I walked in the hallway, I was stopped and asked for a pass. I told them that I was a teacher.

At one point, I went down to the cafeteria to buy lunch, but the cafeteria lady refused to sell lunch to me and kept telling me that I was in the wrong line. I told her that I was a teacher, but she did not believe me.

I went back upstairs to the Teachers' Room and told one of my colleagues, John Martini. He took me to the cafeteria to buy lunch.

I was in line behind him and when I approached the front, he told the lady, "I do not know who this kid is. He followed me in here."

The cafeteria lady told me to get out of the line. John was laughing. Immediately, he told the lady that I was a teacher.

I finally got my lunch.

FOOD WASN'T MY ONLY CHALLENGE, I was teaching three periods a day: US History and Western History and the World, but I did not have my own classroom.

In the history classes, my students were mainly Cambodian students. I worked very closely with the administration on many issues that really didn't have much to do with teaching.

I traveled from classroom to classroom with all of my textbooks and materials on a black audiovisual cart. Durfee High School is a very large building, and I wheeled my books through the halls that were packed by more than two thousand students.

After teaching for three periods, I was assigned to the Fall River Future Office, where I worked collaboratively with other counselors on preventing students from dropping out of high school.

I told my Cambodian students that after I was teaching, I would be in the Future Office, which was located above the library. Many of them came by to talk about their educational plans, their frustrations with school, and the problems that they faced in the school with other students.

33

A NEW JOB WAS NOT MY ONLY CONCERN AS 1990 came to an end. Samoutta and I were also starting a family.

When my wife was pregnant with our first son, those nine months were the most joyful times of our lives. We were looking forward to having him. One weekend, my wife and I drove to Cape Cod, pointing out different scenes to our son. We walked along the beach and I rubbed my wife's belly telling my son how beautiful the world was.

We decided on the name, Makthra Iem Men. Mak – came from my name (MAKna) and Thra came from my wife's name (SamouTTA). He would be our first son. He was special to us.

During her pregnancy, she refused to drink coffee, take Tylenol, or any other medications. She wanted to care for his health, even though he was not born yet. She loved him and she did not want anything to tamper with his health. When she was in her last trimester, we would not go far from the house.

One day, my wife and I were eating pizza at the corner of Atwells and Mt. Pleasant Avenues in Providence, and she told me that she needed to go to the hospital. Our son was on the way.

We rushed out and went to Sturdy Memorial Hospital in Attleboro, Massachusetts. The reason we went there was because my wife's health insurance was in Massachusetts. Our son was born later that night. He was 8 pounds and 21 inches.

MAKTHRA WAS BORN ON JANUARY 7, 1991. He was the most adorable baby I had ever seen. When the doctor handed him to me, I was so afraid that I might drop him. He was my precious son, our first born son.

He looked so adorable and I asked the doctor, "Hold him?"

And he said, "Yes, hold him. He is your son."

I was nervously holding him and kept on looking into his eyes as he cried. The doctor then asked me to cut the umbilical cord and I asked the doctor, "Will this hurt my son and my wife?"

He said, "No."

I cut the cord and now we became three.

When morning came, I went home and told our parents that my wife had delivered a healthy baby boy last night and she was at Sturdy Memorial Hospital in Attleboro. It was a very proud moment.

My wife and I looked at each other and without saying a word, we knew we had a beautiful son. A future! He was loved and would be spoiled by many. My wife and I tried to provide for him with everything that we could afford.

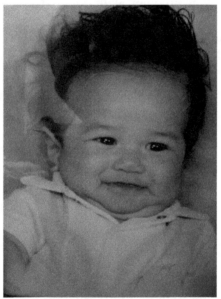

Makthra Men, 2 months old

AFTER SHOWERING AND GETTING A BITE to eat, I was eager to rush back to see my newborn son and wife. When I got back to the room, I noticed the baby sleeping next to my wife did not resemble the baby I saw last night.

My son had a little scratch on his face. I asked my wife when the nurse had brought the baby in to her. She said a while ago. I told her that I did not think this was the right baby. We checked and sure enough, the baby was a girl.

That same night, there was another Cambodian couple who gave birth to a baby girl and the nurse apparently swapped our babies. I immediately ran to the nurse and told her she gave my wife the wrong baby and immediately, the nurse brought my son back.

Since he was the first son, we wanted everything perfect for him. When we brought him home, we lived on 19 Grand Street in Providence, RI.

In that same year, my wife and I bought a house on 78-80 Dorchester Avenue, Providence, RI. We did not have enough money for a down payment on a house, so I borrowed $10,000 from my brother for the down payment and closing cost.

We could not afford a single family home, so we bought a three decker home in Providence so we could generate some rental income to help pay the mortgage. After a few years, my wife and I were able to pay off the $10,000 loan we borrowed.

We wanted to be independent from the family and be on our own. We lived on the second floor and we continued to raise him the best we knew how. We were young and what we had learned was from what we read and what people told us to do. We adored him.

I looked forward to being home and playing with him, but most of the time, he refused to get off his mother. He lay on top of her all the time, watching her and playing with her. He was attached to her when he was home.

Sometimes, I had to take him off from her just to hold him, squeeze him, kiss him and grab onto his chubby cheeks. When he learned to walk, we spoiled him with all kinds of toys. At one point he was trying to get on top of a toy bike and fell. He turned around and kicked the bike and as he cried, he ran to his mother pointing to the toy.

MAKTHRA WAS VERY CLOSE TO HIS MOTHER. His mother breastfed him for many months until she went back to work. Every day and night when an opportunity was given, Makthra lay down on his mother's chest, looked at her face, adored her, even though he was not hungry. He slept on her every opportunity he got.

At night, he refused to sleep in his crib. When his mother put him in, he cried, and as soon as his mother picked him up, he stopped because he knew that he would be laying down on top of her.

We spoiled him to the point that when he was two years old, he needed surgery for his rotten teeth. It was one of the scariest feelings for any parent to go through. He was two years old and they had to put him to sleep to remove his teeth.

He needed dental surgery because we were told that we had him on the bottle too long. We wanted to make sure that he never went hungry. Whatever time, day or night, we gave him milk.

Every day, Makthra learned new words and I was looking forward to seeing him and to playing with him.

My wife even took him to Colorado when he was about two years old. My little son stood on the Rocky Mountains with his unbuttoned coat and posed for a photo.

When my wife showed me the picture, he looked like he was standing so close to the cliff. I was terrified, but my wife assured me that he was not standing close to the cliff.

It was a relief for me.

Makthra on the Rocky Mountains in Colorado, in 1991

WHEN MY WIFE AND I WERE AT WORK, Makthra was cared for by his grandmothers: Tha Chhun and Yan An Iem. His first language was Khmer because he stayed with his grandmothers.

Every night, my wife played soothing melodies for him, to put him to sleep, and to relax him. We treasured him and loved him so much. We provided our son with all the things that both of us never had when we were growing up.

We recorded every move Makthra made in his childhood, including his laugh and his cry. The little things that he did made us laugh with him. We cried with him when he got hurt or when he got sick because he could not tell us what hurt him. We did not want anything to hurt him.

There was not a single day that went by that he was not loved.

SOON, MAKTHRA STARTED PRE-SCHOOL in Fall River Public Schools. Every morning, my son came to school with me.

After a while, it was too much for my son, so we decided to keep him in Providence Schools and he went to West Broadway Elementary School until fifth grade.

From there, he went to Nathaniel Greene Middle School. He was accepted into the Honors program and he stayed until he completed sixth grade. When Makthra entered seventh grade, he was accepted into CVS Highlander Charter School and he stayed there until he graduated from the eighth grade.

34

In 1993, my wife gave birth to our daughter, Marina. Makthra loved his sister, but he did not want to share his mother with her. Every time Marina wanted to lay down on her mother, Makthra refused and cried. He wanted to sleep on his mother and he would not let his little sister sleep on her.

Just like any brother and sister, they became very close. Makthra loved his sister and she loved him as much. I saw their relationship develop fully when Makthra graduated from high school. They were more than siblings. They were best friends.

Our son loved sports, and he was involved in all sports. My wife knew that and when we lived in Providence, Makthra wanted to play baseball but we had no idea where to sign him up.

After talking with several people, we stopped by the community center to inquire about baseball. We found out that there was Little League baseball. None of us knew anything about baseball, but my son wanted to play.

Makthra was interested in playing so we signed him up. We went to the store to buy baseball equipment. We had no idea what to buy, but people at the store helped us. When we got home, I did not know how to play baseball.

My son and I learned to catch a baseball together. We learned how to put the glove on together. It was fun for both of us.

My wife never missed a single game that my son played. I missed some of the games because of work, school and involvement in the Cambodian Community of RI, but I tried to be there for as many games as I could.

Our son soon was selected to play on the All Star team representing the Silver Lake neighborhood. Makthra was proud, his mother was proud, and so was I. He went from not knowing a thing about baseball to the All Stars.

AS THE YEARS WENT BY, I became the "go to" person for many of the challenges and problems that Cambodian students experienced, not just at Durfee High School, but throughout the school district in Fall River, Massachusetts.

Some of the problems of Cambodian students were gang related. They attached themselves to the "reds" and the "blues" and both of these groups were in my classroom. It was difficult to teach them because these groups could not get along.

On top of that, there were also other "groups" in the school and these groups got into fights often. Usually, the fights involved Cambodian students. I was called often to try to figure out what happened and to work with those students.

Although Durfee High School had a diverse population, the students were mostly from a European background. They did not know or understand much about the Asian experience.

My students and I organized Cambodian New Year's celebrations and tried to educate the students and teachers about Southeast Asia. It was a challenge, but we had fun organizing events featuring authentic dance, music and food.

IT WAS DIFFICULT JUGGLING FAMILY and my job, but the work I was doing in Fall River was rewarding. That inspired me to go back to school and earn my Master's Degree in Education.

In 1994, I decided to go to Cambridge College with a colleague from the Futures Office and started a Master's Degree program in Guidance. Every day after work, my colleague and I commuted together to Cambridge, Massachusetts and in 1996, I successfully earned my Master's Degree in Education.

In 1997, a bilingual Guidance Counselor position opened, and I applied for the position. I got the position and I was no longer teaching.

But I had a lot more responsibilities in this new role. I spent half a day at Durfee High School and the other half day in various schools throughout the City of Fall River.

In my new position, I worked with all of the schools in Fall River, Massachusetts. At the time, there was only one high school, but four middle schools and 28 elementary schools.

My duties ranged from translating for parents of special needs Cambodian students in IEP (Individual Educational Plans) sessions for parents, to community outreach, to scheduling building and counseling students about career choice.

The job was much more challenging that I thought. If I had been able to stay in one place, I think it would have been all right, but I was sent around the city and that became very difficult.

Samoutta, Makna and Makthra at the Cambridge College graduation, 1996

35

IN 1997 I LEFT FALL RIVER and accepted a job as a Guidance Counselor in the Providence Public Schools. It was a short commute from home.

During that same year, I met a Cambodian sport team delegation from Cambodia who came to the University of Rhode Island. Although we only met on a few occasions, we kept in contact and became friends.

A year later, I had an opportunity to visit Cambodia and I spent some time travelling with this friend in the country of my birth. On one of those trips, this individual went to see a *Kru Teay* – a fortune teller.

He was a believer in fortune tellers. I only had encountered fortune tellers a few times, when I was desperate, looking for something positive with hope so I could go on with life.

The *Kru Teay* was supposed to be possessed by a young girl from the spiritual world. I was in the back room, and I formed my own opinion as I was listening to my friend's future.

One morning, he asked me to go with him to a spiritual lady who claimed to be "entrenched," or her body possessed by a spiritual world. I went along with him, but mostly for sightseeing and just to get out of the house. I had no transportation and I had no idea where to go.

We arrived at her house, and I could not tell you how long it took because I was not looking forward to meeting the spiritual lady. I was more interested in going out to eat at restaurants, visiting old ruins, and other historical sites.

All of us entered the house and we were directed to the back room. As soon as we entered the back room, the door was locked. I sat in the back of the room by myself, waiting for my new friend and his friends to finish their readings.

The lady lit up the incense, candles, and started chanting. All of a sudden, she spoke in a different voice: a childlike voice. I observed the playfulness of this spirit as she came alive in front of me.

At first, I did not pay too much attention to it and sometimes I ignored it completely. I thought it was a hoax. This is not real, so I thought.

During every moment that I was in that room, I had negative reactions to what the fortune teller said. I did not believe what this person was saying and I was appalled that my friend believed this lady. In fact, I dismissed the whole concept and I thought it was just a money-making business

After an hour or so, it was over and I was looking forward to our next sightseeing trip – or maybe lunch. When we were about to leave, the lady who was supposedly possessed by a spirit from another world called me in.

I refused. But the lady kept asking. So did my new friend and some of his friends in the room. At the end, I gave in because I was trying to be polite and I wanted to avoid an argument.

My new friend kept on pushing me and because I respected him, I moved forward to be read. The fortune teller asked me to show her my left palm and my right palm and I did.

She looked at my face and she looked at my palm again.

IN A PLAYFUL MANNER, the *Kru Teay* started telling me about my life. She said I had five children. At that time in 1998, I only had two, Makthra and Marina. I told her she was wrong and that I had two children.

The spiritual lady kept on saying five and she continued to say that one of those five will go far away from you. I asked her, "How far? Are you talking about moving to another country, moving away from me to somewhere else?"

The spiritual lady replied, "I cannot tell you, it is the secret of life, but all I can tell you is that one will go far away from you."

Marina, Makthra, Kanika and Nicsaii, 2000

THE SECOND THING SHE SAID WAS I would change my job when I got back to the United States. At the time, I was employed as a Guidance Counselor at the Providence Public Schools. It was a city job, a secure job, with summers off and shorter days. In fact, I was the first Cambodian guidance counselor in the City of Providence.

Why would I change my job? Again, I argued with this lady. Since all of what she said were events in the future, I did not pay attention to any of it. This was just to reaffirm my thoughts that it was hoax.

When she came to the third point of my life, she picked up something from my past that no one knew about, not even my mother. She began telling me that at one point around 1976 or 1977, I was very sick and I lost my eyesight. That's when she got my attention.

During the Khmer Rouge time, I was very sick, in fact, I lost my eyesight temporarily. My mother had to carry me on her back all the time and my brother Marin tried to stay with me so other children would not steal my food.

The *Kru Teay* looked at me and said, "Around 1977, you were very sick and there was a little boy who gave you a bowl of water and that water was holy water that you drank."

I asked her to repeat what she said many times, because I did not believe what I heard from this person.

"You lost your eyesight and there was a little boy who came to your bedside and gave you a bowl of water and the water you drank was holy water.

"You have a spiritual person looking after you. That water cured you and saved your life."

This was something that took place a long time ago and I was fearful to disclose this information to anyone, not even my mother. I did not want people to think that I was unstable.

For many years, I had kept what I saw to myself because I could not distinguish in my mind whether it had really happened or if it was a hallucination. For more than 20 years, I never thought my vision could be anything else – until 1998, in this back room at this woman's house.

I was speechless, and amazed at what this lady said to me. She caught my interest and I asked her who was it was that helped me during that time.

Is it possible for me to meet this spiritual world? She called upon the spiritual world and we met.

IT WAS ONE THING TO PREDICT THE FUTURE, but knowing exactly what happened in my past, was creepy and unrealistic. As she was telling me what had happened and what would happen, someone wrote down everything for me. When it was over, the note taker handed me the paper that included the part that said one of my children was going far away from me. I crossed that section out and I kept saying to myself that this would never happen. Nothing that this woman said will ever happen.

At the end of the reading, the lady asked me to come back again the next day and this time, I would be the only one in the room with her. She said she would reveal my future. She said my life had been written; I could not change it.

I did not return to her.

36

I CAME BACK HOME and a new school year started for the Providence Public Schools. Months went by and I was very settled in my job, but it was not very rewarding.

One day, as I was sitting in my office at Central High School, Fran Collignon knocked on my door. She was wondering if I would be interested in going to work for Brown University. I did not jump on it at first.

The position was funded by a federally-funded, five-year grant. Instead of working for the Providence Public Schools as a city employee, my job would be funded by the U.S. Department of Education.

At first I said no, but Fran continued to talk to me about the salary and the benefits Brown offered. I came home that day and I spoke with my wife about the position at Brown University and she encouraged me to take it. I accepted the position and resigned from the Providence Public Schools.

THE EDUCATION ALLIANCE GRANT was for the Southeast Asian career ladder. Basically, the grant was awarded to the Education Alliance to help the Southeast Asians in Rhode Island to pursue a career in teaching in the public schools. I was hired to oversee the Career Ladder program, called Project ADVANCE.

For this particular program, the grant was for fifteen students. The following year, the Education Alliance applied for another grant and it was awarded again for another fifteen students and this time it was called Project IMPACT. I worked with these students throughout the seven years.

There were many challenges, from applying for admission to colleges and universities to job placement. I worked very closely with various Admissions Offices, advocating for students for Admissions

146

and the Dean of the College. At the same time, I also worked closely with Human Resources in various school districts in Rhode Island to keep them informed about the thirty Southeast Asian teachers who would soon be certified to teach in Rhode Island from elementary school to high school.

Besides overseeing the two projects, I also worked with the New England Equity Assistance Center on various issues, such as parental involvement in schools. I often brought the Cambodian cultural perspectives into the discussion. Throughout my seven years at the Education Alliance, I presented many workshops, and spoke at various national and regional conferences throughout the United States, highlighting the success of Project ADVANCE and Project IMPACT.

WHAT THE SPIRITUAL LADY HAD TOLD ME a few months ago, now came true. I changed my job.

But I kept on thinking about her telling me one of my children was going away. I thought that one of my children would have a wonderful job somewhere in the world and move there. That what I was hoping for.

Now, looking back at that piece of paper carefully, when she said it is the secret of life, and she cannot reveal it I now understood what it meant. It meant that my son would die and I never would get to see him again in this lifetime.

In my son's 24 years, he had done so much − far beyond anyone can imagine. His mother gave him the greatest love, unconditional love, as well as to all of us. He was a joy.

SOON AFTERWARD, MAKTHRA HAD TO CHOOSE a high school. Where would he will go? I made a promise to my son that if he passed a Classical High School examination test, I would take him to Cambodia, to see where his mother and I came from. He took the test, passed the test, and was accepted into Classical High School.

The trip to Cambodia never happened. It was the most regrettable memory for me. At the same time, my son also applied to Providence Country Day (PCD) in East Providence and was accepted there.

Makthra wanted to attend PCD. We let him go there, but we had to pay about $5,000 a year. It was a lot of money for us and we were struggling to pay the monthly bill.

When he was at PCD, his mother went to most of his home football games. When the coach put him in, his mother either closed her eyes when someone hit him or she walked away when he was in play. She did not like seeing anyone hitting her son.

IN 2000, MY WIFE GAVE BIRTH to our twins, Kanika and Nicsaii. Vilai Or and Samnang Kea-Or became their Godparents. Not long after, in 2002, my wife's mother, Yan An Iem passed away.

It was devastating to us all. Makthra shaved his head in her honor following the Buddhist tradition. Subsequently, he tattooed his grandmothers' name on his chest.

I also found out from my daughter that he had his friend tattoo a drawing of the Angkor Wat, which he designed himself. I did not know about either of these tattoos.

Also in 2002, our family went on a trip to France. Our trip coincided with the Cambodian New Year so we spent the New Year celebration in Paris.

It was great that our family was there together. Those were the memories that we will cherish forever.

Makthra and Marina in Paris, 2002

IN 2005, WE BOUGHT A HOUSE IN CRANSTON WEST so all our children could attend the Cranston Public Schools. During that same year, I received a Master of Arts degree from Brown University in Development Studies.

But in 2006, the grant for my job at Brown ended and I was looking for another job.

Makthra holds Makna's diploma from Brown University, 2005

37

ONCE AGAIN, I RETURNED TO FALL RIVER. As I was searching for a new opportunity, I saw a job posting at Bristol Community College as Academic Counselor.

The college is located on Elsbree Street not far from Durfee High School. I applied for the position and I got an interview. About two months went by and I got another phone call to come in for the second interview. Subsequently, I was offered the job.

I started out two days a week at the Attleboro Campus and three days at the Fall River campus. I was going back and forth for about two years before the college asked me to take on the Acting Director of Advising position.

It was a challenging job. I was in the position for about ten months before I resigned and went back to my Academic Counselor position.

The college decided to keep me at the Fall River campus five days a week. I became the Advising Center Coordinator, working with part-time and full-time staff and meeting with students throughout the year.

In this role, I worked closely with the Registrar, Admissions, Enrollment Center and the Testing Center, serving thousands of students each year. It was a good fit.

WE TOOK MAKTHRA OUT OF PCD and enrolled him at Cranston West High School where he graduated in 2009. When he was in high school, he played basketball and golf for the school.

When Makthra graduated from high school, it was the proudest moment for us. He was accepted at the University of Rhode Island and was going to attend there in September. Our son was in college.

My wife and I went to his orientation and I walked with my son with pride. Whatever he needed, my wife and I provided for him. My wife and I bought him a brand new car in 2008. We gave it to him as a gift for his success in high school.

The Men Family in 2006

In his senior year, his uncle, Roukha Iem, invited him to go on a seven day cruise. We let him go and when he got on the cruise ship, he called me with happiness. He kept saying, "Dad, the ship is huge and it is all we can eat." I was so happy to hear my son enjoying this time.

Once the cruise ship left the port, I did not hear from him for the next seven days. I waited and waited until that seventh days arrived so I could call him to find out about his trip.

He also got to go to Walt Disney with another uncle, Ka Men. He was happy that he got to go. Anything that we could do and provide, we did.

Makthra posed with his family after graduation
from Cranston West High School, 2009

NOW, OUR SON WAS A MAN. He had grown up and he was moving out to live on campus. In his first semester in college, I spent a lot of time talking to him about college life — what he needed to do to be successful in college. I pushed my son very hard about education, about being a responsible person, and on accountability. He was a man, not a child anymore. I talked to my son about extra responsibility in college, like becoming heavily involved in clubs or any extracurricular activities.

We talked about being focused in school, not staying up late, time management, paying attention to details, planning out the assignments, etc. The first year in college is challenging, especially right out of high school. I was so worried that my son would not adapt to college. I called him almost every week to check on him, to the point that he asked me to leave him alone.

It was difficult and I tried to honor his request. I admit, I am not the easiest person to get along with and I am not a perfect father either. I am strict and I expect my children to follow certain guidelines in life.

As a father, yes, my children have disappointed me, but my love for them is unconditional. I gave my son many lectures about life and sometimes he avoided me because he did not want me to lecture him. I knew that he did a lot in his life, but what I saw in him, he could do more and I never stopped pushing him.

The conversation that my son and I had usually involved how is doing in school and what kinds of friends he was hanging out with. I was not with him 24 hours a day and I always worried.

He told me that he had a lot of influence over his friends. He said to me a few times that because of him, his friends went back to school and straightened out their lives. I was happy to hear that he had that kind of influence, but I also reminded him that he had to help himself. He replied, "I know Dad."

Makna and Samoutta celebrate with Makthra
after his graduation from YEAR UP

AFTER MAKTHRA GRADUATED from Bristol Community College (BCC), he said he wanted to go on to get his Bachelor's Degree. At one point, my son wanted to enroll at Eastern Nazarene College and he and I got everything ready.

My son and I went through the financial aid process and he did not get any aid. My son and I talked about him attending there and I told him that I would pay half for him and he could take out a loan for the other half. I believe the total cost would be around $10,000.

Makthra did not want to take the $5,000 I offered him. He said he wanted to do this on his own. I let him be.

Soon afterward, I gave him information on an articulation agreement with Wentworth Institute of Technology and Bristol Community College. He immediately jumped on that opportunity.

Since he was a little boy, he always wanted to be a Project Manager. Wentworth offered a Bachelor's Degree program at BCC campus in Project Management.

He enrolled in the program and he was on his way. He completed the first semester and started the second. With all the credits he earned at BCC, he almost completed the first two years of the Project Management program.

Makthra Men and family at his 2013 graduation from BCC.

38

MAKTHRA GREW UP on Dorchester Avenue, which was where our first home in Providence was located. When he got older, he wanted to move back there, and so we agreed.

He moved in in October of 2014 and whenever I visited him there, he told me to take off my shoes. He wanted to keep his house clean.

Before he moved in, my wife wanted to fix the house. It took us a few months to get it ready. We put in a new kitchen floor, new bathroom, new windows and fresh new paint, which he helped put on the walls and ceilings.

Makthra said that he loved the house. Everything was new. He moved his bed in, but the box spring was too big and could not fit in the hallway. My wife and I went shopping and got him a split box spring.

One evening after work, I went to pick it up and moved it in for him while he was at work. I set up his bed, with the headboard facing east, but when he returned from work, he moved his headboard so that it was facing west.

I told him that in our tradition, the headboard should face east or other directions except the west, but he said he loved to have his headboard facing west.

My wife planned to get him a small kitchen dining table and she sent him a picture to see if he liked it. None of it happened.

TIME IS OF THE ESSENCE, I've learned. Each year, my son and I played golf together once or twice a year. When we were on the golf course, we competed. One of his friends from PCD invited us often to play golf on their course. We never got to complete the eighteen holes, but we had a lot of fun.

Sometimes, my son went with his friend and he told me that after the games, they cooked him delicious food. He enjoyed that so much.

In the past year, I took a day off from work so that I could go fishing with him and one night, we went squid fishing together. He caught a few squids and I did not catch any.

On Thanksgiving Day and Christmas Day in 2014, Makthra wanted to compete with me on Ping Pong. I told him that you know you cannot beat me in this game. I used to play this game in college, but he said, "Let's go dad. Let's go."

And we did. We played until my shoulder hurt and I could not play anymore. I hate to say, my son did not beat me in Ping Pong.

Whenever he was at the house, my wife always asked me to take family pictures, so I am not in most of them because I took the pictures. In almost all of the pictures that I took of my son, his left eye was always dimmed, like he was always sleepy. I asked him, and he did not know why.

Whenever he was home, he brought joy to his siblings. They missed him - his goofy smile, tattering steps up the stairs, and the nice hair cut he had. He always brought smiles to his siblings.

Makthra and Marina in 2014

IN EARLY JANUARY OF 2015, my wife decided to have an early birthday for our son and we invited some of his close friends over for dinner. My wife asked me to order a cake for him.

I have never done anything like this before. I called one of my colleagues at work and asked her to place an order for me. She asked if I wanted a half sheet or full sheet cake and I had no idea what either of them looked like. I asked my colleague to order a full sheet cake for me.

After work, I went to pick it up and I was short 60 cents. The bakery did not accept credit cards, but a nice lady behind me gave the 60 cents. I was so embarrassed.

When I went home, I realized that I forgot to get the birthday candles. When the moment came to light the candles, I lit up the Yankee Candle jar and held it over the cake for my son to blow out

We sang Happy Birthday to him. I think that was the highlight of my son's night. His dad held a candle over his cake and had him blow it out.

Makthra's birthday cake.

HOLIDAYS WERE SPECIAL FOR MAKTHRA. In my son's twenty-four years, he never missed a Christmas Day at the house. He enjoyed spending times with his siblings and his parents. I enjoyed seeing his happiness when he was there with his siblings.

On Thanksgiving Day, after he ate, he would often go out in front of the house to play football with his brother, cousins, and friends. Afterwards, he would often take his siblings to the movies.

During all of those holidays, he was always well dressed, and always ready with a smile. He enjoyed my wife's cooking and he told her that, "I love your food Mom."

On any special occasion at the Buddhist temple, Makthra was there, participating in the temple events. Whenever he came across any older person, whether at the mall or on the street or at the temple, he raised both of his hands to greet them.

Everyone that my wife and I knew in the community talked very highly of our son. He was a very respectful and lovely person. We are all going to miss him.

A FEW WEEKS BEFORE HIS ACCIDENT, he asked his mother to cook "hot pot" at his home. This is a special Cambodian dish involving cooking and sharing a meal together. On March 1, 2015, my wife and my daughter decided to have a hot pot at his home.

My daughter invited a lot of his close friends to the house to fulfill his wish. They cooked and they ate.

When he was working at BJ's Headquarters, he said that he did not like the hours because he did not have the weekends off.

It was tough for him.

My son often told me that he was looking for other jobs that had regular hours. I often emailed my friends who worked in the computer field and asked them if they could help my son.

I was told the nature of working as support staff in the computer field was that there was not set hours. I talked to my network of friends and tried to get my son a different job, closer to home.

In fact, on the Friday before his accident, I spoke with two people about my son looking for a job in the computer field.

Whenever my son applied for a job, he called me to let me know that he put the application in. He put application in for jobs in Boston, with Alex and Ani, at Citizens Bank, and others. We talked about those jobs.

Sometimes, I sent him links to jobs and at one point, my son and I filled out job applications together while we were in his house. He kept me informed because he wanted me to know that he was trying to move up.

Makthra wanted to make me proud of him and he wanted to be a responsible, mature person. That was the conversation my son and I had often and I told him that once he completed his study at Wentworth Institute of Technology, he could move up and move out to other positions.

I told him to be patient and he would get to his dream job. He was mature and I was proud of him.

Makthra looks toward a bright future, 2015

39

TAKE YOUR TIME. One thing that I always reminded my children, both Makthra and Marina, was to go slow when they were driving. I am sure they were tired of hearing me. Whenever my children went to school or work, my worries began. In the back of my mind, I was always thinking of their safety.

One evening when I was driving home from work in January of 2015, my son called me and said:

"Daddy, I want to let you know that I love you and mom and that you have raised a good son. I appreciate what you have done for me and I understand what you have said to me all along. I won't disappoint you."

I cried and I told my son:

"Son, Daddy loves you too and I appreciate it very much what you just said to me. All Daddy wants for you is for you to have a great future. I want you to have something better then what Daddy is having now."

I was choked up and I could not talk to my son because his words meant so much to me.

It heals my heart that my son acknowledged my teachings. Sometimes, I think I am involved in my children's lives too much. I wanted so much for them that I may have neglected their feelings that they grew up in the United States and the upbringing in this culture is different than the one I grew up in.

This is the reason that I think that I may have not been a perfect father. But from my son's words, I know that any negative things that were said, back and forth, are meaningless.

How lucky was I to hear my son's acknowledgement two weeks before he got into a car accident that took his life? Is this Karma or is this the destiny?

My son gave me the gift to go on in life, by letting me know how much he appreciated me. In that same sentence he said that he loved his mother. I got to hear his words. That was my son.

Makthra never died in my heart. He remains in my heart and soul forever. Occasionally, I feel my son's presence, and I talk to him and let him know that we all loved him. But at the same time, I am also letting him know that he has to move on in his world.

In past years, when there was snow, my wife and I always reminded him to take the four wheel drive vehicle to work and if there was a lot of snow, stay at a motel and do not try to come home. On January 24, 2015, it was snowing and I did not tell him to take the four wheel drive.

This is something I have regretted tremendously. I ask myself again and again, "Why didn't I tell him to take the car?" If he took the car, would he still be alive?

This is something that I will never find out in this lifetime, and it is something that I have to live with.

MAKTHRA LOVED TO HELP PEOPLE. He put everyone else's needs before his. He got that trait and learned that gratitude from his mother. This is the best quality that cannot be taught. It is inside the heart and mind.

My son spent time in soup kitchens, served meals to the homeless community, was involved in community services, either with the temples or community organizations. If he could do anything to help, he was there.

He taught math in the Summerbridge program, and earned a minimum stipend. He was offered a job, but he refused to take it; instead, he wanted to teach other children who were about the same age as him.

After he completed the Summerbridge Program, Makthra kept in touch with the program and continued to support it, and volunteer there. My son had a big heart and his heart touched so many lives.

Everyone who he came across loved him unconditionally. He was polite to the elders and he respected people. His mother taught him to help others, to respect others and to help people in need. He lived up to his mother's teachings and expectations.

At his wake, more than 1,500 people showed up to pay their respect and every one of them said Makthra touched their lives and changed their lives. Many of us, living until an old age, would not have touched so many lives. But our son did.

THIS WORLD IS CRUEL. God is cruel to me, to my family and to my son. My son finally understood his life, but it was taken away. He understood what I said to him.

Like one of my friends said to me, you build a house and start it from the foundation. You dig a hole and you pour the cement in. Once the foundation is strong, you start with the frame, and eventually you put on the roof. Once your house is completed and you are ready to move in, it burns down.

You did not get to enjoy it. You did not get to see what was inside of this house. You did not get a chance to decorate it.

My son called me and said to me that he appreciated what I had done for him. He understood what I had been saying to him all this time. I did not get to see how my son would have turned out to be. I lost my future.

In his short life, my son grew up to be a man. He understood life, but my wife and I did not get to see his full potential as a man.

Makthra had great plans for his life. He kept telling me that he would not disappoint me and that he planned to retire at 35 or so. He kept saying that he had a plan, and he asked that I wait and see his plan.

He mentioned his plan to his sister, Marina, many times, but he would not reveal what it was.

Our family lost a future. As I am writing this memoir of my beloved son, tears roll down my eyes and sadness takes over. Confusion and anger prevail. My son left his family ten months ago, and the sorrow and pain persist in my heart each day. There is not a single day and hour that goes by without me thinking of him. Sometimes, I catch myself looking for him in the house. So many times, that I wanted to yell out his name, looking for him, and catching myself asking my wife or my children to find him in the house so he can come to eat dinner. Son, where are you? Why did you leave us?

In Memoriam

Makthra I. Men, 24, of Council Rock Rd., Cranston, passed away on Saturday, January 24, 2015 at U. Mass Medical Center in Worcester. Born in Attleboro, MA, he was the devoted son of Makna and Samoutta (Iem) Men.

Makthra was an I.T. in the computer technology industry. He was a 2009 graduate of Cranston High School West where he was a member of the basketball team and golf team. During the summer, he would volunteer his time with the students at Breakthrough Providence / Summerbridge at Wheeler. He also donated his time in soup kitchens and with Cambodian Society.

He received his Associate Degree from Bristol Community College and was attending Wentworth Institute of Technology. He was a recent graduate of the Year Up Program. Makthra played little league baseball in Silver Lake and was elected an All Star and enjoyed football, basketball and golf.

Besides his parents, he was the loving brother of Marina Men, Kanika Men and Nicsaii Men, all of Cranston.

40

MY WIFE AND I HAVE DIFFERENT MEMORIES of our son. I was tough on my son. My wife was tough on him as well, but with a lot of compassion. I did not show as much compassion toward my son, but my love for my son was tough love.

My compassionate love for my son and for all my children tends to be more inside and within. I expect all of my children to be successful and my expectations sometimes overshadow the reality of life.

Occasionally, I called my son and reminded him to go slow when I did not see him. Once in a while, he stopped by BCC, where I work now, and surprised me with his lady.

Again, before he left me, I reminded him of going slow and his response was, "I know Dad."

Sometimes, I also reminded my son to save money when he could because you never know when you will need it. He often let me know that he knew and I did not have to remind him all the time.

My wife often reminded me to let them be; they are good children. I do not disagree with her, but it is very difficult for me not to remind them of certain things in life.

Sometimes the conversations that I had with my son were only to remind him of doing certain things. I always told him, to be successful in life, there is no other way around it, except education.

Makthra and his mother, Samoutta.

I MISS MY SON DEARLY. I miss his goofiness, his competitiveness, his smile, his ability to persuade others, his outspoken opinion against injustice, his ability to see beyond what was in front of him, his voluntarism, his care for others, his love for his mom and siblings, his respectfulness towards elders and his ability to communicate across the spectrums, and so much more.

From this point forward, my life will never be the same and I am sure that my wife's and my children's lives will be never the same.

Losing a child is one of the most treacherous emotional experiences anyone could imagine. There are many sleepless nights, and sometimes I feel that I am going to have a heart attack, sometimes I cannot breathe, and my body aches everywhere.

At times, I felt that the world came to an end. I could not care less what took place around me. I just wanted to sleep. For days and days, I am tired, weak, and any activities that I enjoyed doing, like fishing and golf, have come to a halt.

My world may feel like it has ended for me, but I am sure that my son Makthra does not want to see me like this.

YES, THERE WERE REGRETS in this lifetime, but I did not know that my son had only 24 years of life with me and his family. If I had known that my son would live only 24 years, things would have been different, but that's the mystery of life.

No one can predict when and where life will end. In this lifetime, whenever that life will end for me, I will always wonder what would have happened if I had done certain things.

Would anything I did have changed my son's future?

There will always be questions in my mind, head and heart. Why did I do certain things and did not accept certain things from my son? Did I love him enough? Did I spend enough time with him? Did I accept his failures or successes? Did I praise him enough? Where did I go wrong or right?

These are the questions to which I will never know the answers, and they will be with me forever. I hope that when I die, I will see him again and those questions will be answered.

It is my hope - and that is all I have left – that I will be a better father for my other three children, Marina, Kanika and Nicsaii.

The Men Family in happier times.

In July of 2015, 10 chairs were made and donated to an elementary school in Cambodia in memory of Makthra Iem Men.

Clean Water, a Human Right not a Luxury

Water for Cambodia

Water for Cambodia began as a Rotarian project. According to their website, Donations and grants help the group build and install biosand water filters, household units that produce clean drinking water directly from contaminated sources. An estimated 15,000 filters now bring clean water to more than 90,000 people.

*In the summer of 2015, Makna and Nicsaii travelled to Cambodia
to stencil water filters in Makthra's memory.*

Epilogue

In our belief, life has a pre-determined ending date that is unknown to us. Lord Buddha has given us a life on earth to fulfill our obligations – whatever those obligations are.

The life we have is determined by our previous life, and the acts of our current life will determine our next life. The acts of kindness and helping others in need will benefit this life and the next life as long as our act is pure and honest.

Lying and stealing from other people's hard work to benefit yourself is not pure; therefore, your act of kindness towards other is not pure because you have committed an act of dishonesty. The benefit cannot be passed on from oneself to another.

People in my community, along with Buddhist Monks have said many times to me and to my family that my son Makthra was born to fulfill his obligations from previous life. He was given to me for 24 years to learn about life.

Lord Buddha had a bigger plan for him.

We taught him about life and he understood it. Makthra called me a few weeks before his tragic car accident that took his life and he said to me, "Dad, you have raised a good son."

And then he said:

"I understood what you have said to me. Thank you and I love you."

Was that my son's unconscious mind that spoke to me and expressed those precious words to me? Is our life really pre-determined?

I have tried to come up with an explanation, but I cannot come up with any. But analyzing this life helps keep my mind in check.

THAT BRINGS ME TO MY OWN LIFE. What was my previous life like?

I lived through battlefields in Cambodia with the Khmer Rouge, and the refugee camps before resettling in the United States. There were many lessons in life.

Were those lessons in life meant for me to teach my own children?

I have taught my children of the hardships. I have taught my children the value of helping others in need and the less fortunate.

For many years, my friends, family and I have contributed to the Water for Cambodia project. I remember how precious water was when my family made our journey to freedom.

In 2015, according to the Water for Cambodia website, more than 50% of the rural Cambodian population still does not have access to safe drinking water and about 20% of the deaths of children under five are due to waterborne diseases.

In addition to teaching the Cambodian people how to use and maintain the filters, Water for Cambodia provides basic instruction in hygiene, as well as reading, writing and math.

Since 2011, my colleagues at Bristol Community College have raised money for Water for Cambodia. During the summer of 2015, Nicsaii and I went to the Water for Cambodia's headquarter in Siem Reap, Cambodia.

It was my son's second trip to our homeland, but it was his first time to Water for Cambodia's headquarters, and it was a journey in remembrance of Makthra.

As part of the project, we stenciled Makthra's name on three filters. It seemed an appropriate way to try to calm the rough waters of loss and sadness.

Although it has not brought complete calm, it is good to know that in a small way, the circle is complete. We left Cambodia surrounded by death, but returned with a gift of life, water. This is a tribute to my beloved son, Makthra. He would have wanted his family to continue to give and to help others in need.

Learn this from water:
Loud splashes the brook
but the oceans depth are calm.
- Buddha

Bibliography

Heaton, Donald. D. *A Consumer's Guide on World Fruit.* North
 Charleston: BookSurge, 2006.
Potash, Wayne. "Leak Kanseng." *Yes! Wayne Potash*, 2014.
 http://waynepotash.com/leak-kanseng

174

About the Authors

Makna Men currently works at Bristol Community College as Senior Academic Counselor. He also continues to provide technical assistance to community-based organizations. Makna has also presented at Regional and National Conferences on issues related to race, gender and national origin.

This book tells the story of his escape from Cambodia and resettlement in Rhode Island, where he graduated from Central High School and went on to Rhode Island College, where he obtained a BA in Social Science/Secondary Education; Cambridge College, earning a Masters of Education in Guidance Counseling; and a Master of Arts in Development Studies from Brown University.

Inspired by these events to help others, Makna became involved with the Cambodian Society of RI (CSRI), Inc. as a volunteer in the early 1980s. Makna taught the Khmer language and participated in other activities sponsored by the CSRI. Makna continued to participate as a board member and advisor for eight years. In the 1990s, along with the CSRI's President, he secured a $50,000 Block Grant from the City of Providence to purchase a building on Hanover Street for a community center.

In 1989, Makna was a co-founder of the Asian Student Association at Rhode Island College, and in the late 1990s, Makna worked with staff from the Providence Children's Museum to create an exhibit about his wedding at the Museum in an effort to teach children about Cambodian culture. It was on display until February of 2006.

In 2002, Makna was appointed by the Mayor of Providence to a three year term for the Providence School Board. When Makna left the School Board, he joined Project AIDS Khmer in RI, and was elected to a post to direct their public relations. For the last four years, Makna has been involving in organizing Water for Cambodia fund raising events.

Makna taught at BMC Durfee High School in Fall River, Massachusetts for six years before becoming a guidance counselor. Subsequently, Makna took a new position in the Providence Schools where he became the first guidance counselor from the Southeast Asian communities.

Makna left the Providence School district to work at the Education Alliance at Brown University in 1998 where he worked in the areas of access to education and teacher quality. He also coordinated two Southeast Asian Career Ladder Programs with thirty pre-service and in-service teachers participating.

Makna lives in Cranston with his wife, Samoutta, and three children, Marina and twins, Kanika and Nicsaii. Their son Makthra died in a car accident in 2015. This is Makna's first book.

Michael J. Vieira, Ph.D. retired in 2013 as Associate Vice President of Academic Affairs at Bristol Community College, where he also served as Dean of the Division of Business and Information Management and acted in other leadership positions. Prior to his move into administration, Mike served as a full-time member of the Computer Information Systems Department and continues to teach for BCC, Wentworth Institute of Technology, Easter Nazarene College and other schools.

For more than 20 years, he taught in Fall River's public schools and advised the student publications at B.M.C. Durfee High School. Since 1974, he has been published regularly in area newspapers including the *Standard-Times* and the Providence and magazines including SouthCoast Insider and *Prime Times*.

Mike has written and edited a number of books including *A History of Camp Noquochoke*, a Boy Scout Camp in Westport, MA, *100 Years of Student Journalism* in Fall River, *A Brief History of Wareham* published by The History Press, and *The Blessing: Ghosts of Gage Hill* which was written by his Durfee classmate Deborah Correia Romano and her family. He is currently working with J. North Conway on a book about New England rock formations. It will be published by The History Press in 2016.

A graduate of Bridgewater State College (B.A. and M.A.T.), he holds a Certificate of Advanced Graduate study from Rhode Island College and earned his doctorate in Education at Capella University. A native of Fall River, he now lives in Swansea with his wife, Audrey. They have two children and their first grandchild, Kyle Michael.